MISFITS ABROAD

ADVENTURES IN LOVE, LANGUAGE AND FOREIGN LANDS

MARTINE ROBINSON BEACHBOARD

Livingwell Publishing

TAOS, NEW MEXICO, USA

Livingwell Publishing
ATTN: Permissions Coordinator
1417 Santa Cruz Road
Taos, New Mexico 87571 USA
www.livingwellpublishing.com

Book Layout based on BookDesignTemplates.com
Book Cover by Natalia Larguier

"Emmène-Moi Demain Avec Toi" written by L. & P. Sebastian and Michaële
"Il Me Faut Vivre" music by Christian Bruhn; French lyrics by Ralph Bernet
"L'Homme Qui Sera Mon Homme" written by Jean-Loup Dabadie, Olivier Toussaint, and Paul de Senneville
"Pardonne-Moi Ce Caprice d'Enfant" written by Patricia Carli
"Big Chill" screenwriters: Lawrence Kasdan and Barbara Benedek (1983)

For privacy reasons, names, locations, and dates have been changed.
Misfits Abroad: Adventures in Love, Language and Foreign Lands / Martine Robinson Beachboard – 1st ed.
ISBN (Paperback Edition) 979-8-9915191-0-6
ISBN (Hardback Edition) 979-8-9915191-0-7
ISBN (Print Edition, Barnes & Noble) 979-8-9915191-2-0
ISBN (eBook) 979-8-9915191-3
Library of Congress Control Number: 2024918882

CONTENTS

*Dedicated to everyone I love in Europe —
particularly those with a sense of humor — and
to all those friends who kept saying, When are
you going to write a book?*

ACKNOWLEDGMENTS

Thank you to Dennis Wurst, Patricia Herrewig,
James Herrewig, Susanne Forrest,
Richard A. Smith, Daniel Mintie, and
Wick Communications.

INTRODUCTION

The collection of stories presented here introduces colorful people and places I encountered when I left my sheltered, little hometown and moved to Europe. Vignettes center on the time I spent living and working with military communities in Germany and traveling further abroad. A new environment in the Old World broadened my perspectives. It is my hope that these stories will enrich your life too.

MOVING ABROAD

....

AU REVOIR, AUF WIEDERSEHEN

When Pamela moved to France, I plopped down on the kitchen floor and sobbed into my bowl of red-flavored Jell-O. I was five and Pam was three, and her family was going away forever. While Mother was a little sad and a good deal envious, I was devastated. Pamela's mom said they would leave me her toy piano, probably so it could drive my mother crazy instead of her.

One of the hardest things about growing up in an army gate town was the continual departure of people I'd grown attached to. Year in, year out, the active-duty families came and went with the call of their fathers to serve in another part of the country or world. As a child, I couldn't understand why friends I loved kept leaving. But they did. Military or civil servant. Active duty or retired. One by one, they left for new experiences and adventures.

Curly-haired Sandy helped me stop crying when I had to ride the school bus in second grade. We held hands on the playground every day until her father took a job in Alamogordo, New Mexico. Virginia came from Brazil, and our fourth-grade teacher worked diligently to get her to say she [mopt] the floor instead of she [mop-ped] it. Virginia would walk me to her house on School Drive and offer me snacks, while her father was studying at the military intelligence school. Then she and her parents went back to São Paulo. Simon sat next to me cracking bilingual jokes in French class until he and his parents left for Lakenheath, England. Russel helped me practice clarinet until his father retired, and they moved to Michigan.

One by one, they left. It was never my turn. My Dad was a civilian with a secure job, so we weren't going anywhere.

Nearly as painful as the departures was the realization that my friends didn't seem to mind the impending separation as much as I did. It took me a long time to learn why. The party who's leaving has the easier lot because she has so many things to do, so much on her mind: packing and passports, new places, new faces, decisions to make. She's thinking hopefully about her future, while my mind cuts an ever-deepening channel in a gully full of memories.

Childhood recollections like making doll food out of mulberries. Fashioning outfits for Wishnik trolls. Melting smelly Crayons on the stove so the dolls could have their own candles. (Got in trouble for that.) Swinging so high that the swing-set posts began pulling out of the ground. Trying on silly hats.

Grown-up memories like helping Henry use boulders to build the Great Retaining Wall of China in his backyard. His daughter, Amy, toddling behind him on what he referred to as her "tree-trunk legs." No more of Grace's appetizer trays loaded with colorful bell peppers. No more

4

commiserating over husbands late to dinner. Their life's new opportunities would leave a gap in my routine.

The farewells cease to be earthshaking, but they're never easy. If the setting happens to be an airport, the event is simplified by a metallic voice announcing the last call to board Flight 404, and you have no choice but to give a quick hug and turn away, hiding eyes filled with tears.

When the parting moments occur at home, it's a little more awkward. There's no outside source to say it's time to go now. Rather, there comes a moment late in the evening when the quiet reminiscing lulls, when the promises to write have been made and repeated, and the kidding around, slightly forced and unnatural sounding, finally dies away.

That's how it was when Henry and Grace moved to Germany. Little farewell speeches hung in the air, unspoken. We all grew silent. Our eyes refused to meet. It seemed like there should be one thing left to say, some final wisdom to impart, but none of it could quite be put into words. Except for these: Goodbye. We'll miss you.

Will it ever be my turn to leave?

⸙

SOME ENCHANTED EVENING

Emmène-Moi Demain avec Toi

Strains of French music flowed from the little black record my grandmother had sent for Christmas. The singer dreams of traveling to exotic islands and far-away cities.

While my contemporaries were listening to the Dave Clark Five and the Association, I lay on the carpeted floor of my peach-and-cream hued bedroom, listening to French singer Mireille Mathieu. The vinyl discs played at 33 RPM but were the size of American 45's. There were two tracks on each side, and I listened to the four songs over and over again, picking up a word here, a phrase there, and trying to learn the French my mother had neglected to teach me.

A long triangular window let in light across the top of the room, following the slant of the ceiling. Against the brilliant azure sky of Southern Arizona, branches of a giant willow tree beat restlessly in the March wind. Outside the narrow, vertical window by the bed, I could see a fraction of the life going on in our middle-class American neighborhood. Two houses across the street, a pale-green one and a white one. They were tract houses like ours, and the same houses I looked at from first grade through high

6

school. The cat lazing in the sun or meowing to get back inside. The postman bringing the Saturday mail and pausing to drink the glass of ice water my mother always prepared, covered with a waxed paper bag and set on the mailbox. Maybe bringing a letter from the other side of the world.

Growing up in America, any rendering of the globe that I saw depicted the Western Hemisphere in a nice, neat circle. That round map was like the "heads" side of a coin. It showed half of planet Earth, centering on America, a creature with its neck stretching up the coast of New England and its forepaws reaching down to the Florida Keys. It even had hind legs, if you included Baja California. Most of the world's land mass and 80 percent of its population were relegated to the "tails" side of the coin, not shown in U.S. popular media. All of Europe and Asia were hidden like the back side of the moon unless you flipped the coin. I wanted to see the flip side.

Mother whisked into the room carrying freshly ironed blouses and home-sewn dresses.

"You're wearing that record out," she remarked. She was not quite five feet tall and not even a hundred pounds, with dark hair threatening to turn gray. Every gesture was quick and energetic, every word short and clipped, with what my friends said was a French accent although I could scarcely detect it.

"I'm glad you're furthering your *français, ma chérie,* but aren't you sick and tired of listening to the same thing

7

repeatedly?" She must have written *Mémé* an urgent request because, shortly thereafter, several new records arrived in a slightly crushed package with royal-blue stickers, fancy stamps, and swirly handwriting. My repertoire widened.

"Il me faut vivre."

The songstress envisions her future love. She has to go and live her own life now.

The vague idea of a junior year abroad or a post-graduation summer in Europe had never materialized, for reasons of practicality and perhaps timidity. Instead, I lay on the bedroom floor, listening to a favorite French singer. When will be my time for adventure?

"Emmène-moi demain avec toi," she pleaded. Tomorrow when you go, take me with you.

~!~

ADVENTURES WITH PASSPORTS

Here we were, embarking on the greatest adventure of our lives, moving to Europe, and it looked like we might have to travel separately. If I didn't receive my passport before my husband left for Germany, I'd have to wait for it and travel later by myself. I already had a blue U.S. tourist passport. What I needed was the official maroon version that would allow me to board a military aircraft. You can't get one without submitting the other, the post travel office informed us. I'd get them both back eventually, but I was running out of time. If I sent off the blue one, and neither was ready on our official departure day, I wouldn't be able to take a military flight without a maroon passport or a commercial flight without a blue one. Surely there must be a record in Washington, D.C. of my having been previously issued a valid passport. Why did they need to see the physical document? They had issued it. The Fort Huachuca travel office assured me it was impossible to accomplish this any other way.

Hmmm. Could I call Uncle Sam? A white Trimline telephone hung on the wall above the built-in kitchen desk. It had a long, springy cord that let me to pace back and forth in the kitchen and out into the living room as I waited for the operator to give me a number for the U.S. Government. That led me to the State Department, which, in turn, took me to the Bureau of Consular Affairs. A few calls and a few minutes later, I found myself speaking with a woman who said, yes, she was able to identify me and verify that I did have valid credentials. She agreed that she could have my official document created and sent to the travel office without her having my blue passport in hand.

In a matter of days, the post travel authorities were phoning John's office. "We didn't handle an application for this," the bureaucrat said with wonder in her voice, "but we seem to have a government passport here for your wife."

⤙⦙⤚

JUMP-STARTING A RABBIT

America no longer had troops in France, so John was not able to transfer to the land of my ancestors. Germany was about as close as we could get. Mother's relatives were a mere six-hour train trip away from where we would be stationed, so she found some consolation in that.

Wanting to have our automobile when we got to our new residence, we had to deliver it to a U.S. port for shipment. So, we drove three-quarters of the way across the United States to send our little yellow Volkswagen Rabbit from South Carolina back to its country of origin.

Because I had just left my parents, I cried for the first two days and refused to look out the windows, but all I missed was west Texas, and that landscape would make a person cry anyway.

By the time we crossed the Mississippi River, I was calm, alert, and ready to start my foreign language study. Workbook in hand, I began reading aloud to John, who already knew some German. It was easy to recognize English cognates in the target language: *mann, hand, finger, haar, schule.*

When we reached the Chattahoochee River, I had made my peace with nouns having not one or two but three genders.

When we were passing beneath Georgia kudzu, I was learning that German, like Greek, could play with word order thanks, in part, to noun case declensions. I began to appreciate my French friend's joke about a man listening to a German political speech. His buddy shows up and asks, "How long has the Chancellor been speaking?"

"About twenty minutes."

"*Ach so.* What's he talking about?"

"I don't know. He hasn't reached a verb yet."

Studying our way across the country, we toured splendid yet controversial plantations in Georgia and eventually reached Charleston, which beguiled us with its antebellum architecture. A charming little lady, wearing authentic period dress, told us how local chinaware sales had suffered when Yankees refused to buy. How white southerners had cleaned their silver and polished their own shoes after dark, because they were ashamed of having to do these menial tasks for themselves. She showed us houses built close together but with windows only on one side, "a southern courtesy" to protect neighbors' privacy. A horse-drawn carriage took us to the point where, as our guide described it, the Ashley and Cooper Rivers joined to form the Atlantic Ocean.

At the Charleston Port of Embarkation, we turned in our vehicle. It would ride for weeks on the deck of a ship crossing the Atlantic in winter.

To reclaim it in Germany, we would take our first train ride, way up north to Bremerhaven. This mode of transportation lived up to my romantic notions as we traveled 600 kilometers, crossing two-thirds of the length of the country and seeing some of its best-known landmarks. The railroad conductor, dressed in a double-breasted, navy-blue uniform and cap, blew his whistle, and the doors slammed shut. The scene was straight out of an old black-and-white movie, and I was instantly enchanted.

We passed Mainz, home of the Gutenberg Museum; the Mouse Tower where the Rhine River bends north at Bingen; the 400-foot slate Lorelei, famous for what another passenger called, in his German accent, the fabled "seven wirgins" whose siren songs sent sailors to their deaths in the rocky waters below.

Near Koblenz, at the confluence of the Rhine and Moselle Rivers, I was agape at the corduroy rows of steep vineyards spanned by the country's largest cable car. Passing such an abundance of lush greenery nearly exploded the rods and cones of this desert gal's eyeballs.

The railway took us through Bonn, the provisional capital of Germany. Then through Cologne, where the train stopped right in front of a thirteenth century Gothic cathedral.

Already I was beginning to realize what a privilege it was to be in Europe.

We went past Düsseldorf and onward toward the North Sea, where the landscape flattens out. Finally, we made it to Bremerhaven, the port from which my mother had left Europe to come to America after World War II. She had given me a black-and-white picture of herself dressed in a civilian uniform consisting of sweater and pleated skirt; she was standing in front of a red-brick barracks. Armed with this little deckled-edge photo, we tried in vain to find that same building so John could photograph me there. Eventually we gave up the search and got a ride to our lodging.

We'd been advised that if we wanted a shower in our hotel room, we needed to specifically request it. So, we did. *Ein Zimmer mit Dusche, bitte.* The room did indeed have the promised shower. In a drab, square little room, set against the middle of one wall, was a shower stall. No separate room, wall, or privacy screen. Just a lonely, naked little shower cabin with a thin aluminum floor that made an atrocious racket when the water hit it. There was no bathroom. The toilet was in the shared water closet down the hall. Well... we hadn't asked for a toilet.

To get your car back, you take a taxi to the port. You visit a little building at the edge of a huge parking lot. You do some paperwork, retrieve your key, run around trying to find your vehicle, start it up, drive back to the office, and do additional paperwork.

Hundreds of cars are parked in long rows under gray skies. We locate our dingy little hatchback at the top of a gently sloping row. Though it is covered with 4,000 miles worth of grease, grime, and salt, it's a welcome sight. John is in a rush to liberate our thoroughly filthy vehicle before the base office closes for the weekend.

We toss our little suitcase in the back. He pulls out the key and jumps into the driver's seat. It won't start. Long, cold trip. Probably a dead battery. It's a manual transmission. We can push start it, he says. I'm to steer as he pushes the VW out of its space and into the wide aisle at the top of the parking lot.

My role is to put the car into second gear and press the clutch while John pushes from behind. We're lucky to have a gentle downhill to work with. When it's going about 5 mph, I'm to release the clutch and then the engine will start. Except it doesn't. That's OK; try it again.

"Pop the clutch!" Nothing.

An explanation of what "pop the clutch" means.

Try again. Nothing.

We keep repeating the process while running out of slope. John has no desire to turn the car around and push it back up the hill to try to start it. I press the brakes but he's still pushing. And getting exasperated.

"Don't you know how to pop the clutch?"

We're nearly at the little checkout office now, and he decides he'll have to do the job all by himself. Open the door, push off with his left foot on the ground and his right foot on the clutch. Go!

Nothing.

As it turned out, there was no electrical connection because a battery clamp had snapped during the frigid transatlantic trip. That vehicle was never going to start without some greater intervention. Shortly before 1630 hours, which was closing time on this Friday afternoon, a security guard offered to drive us to a PX to buy auto parts. And tools, since those had been stolen from the trunk.

Finally, the little Rabbit was liberated, and we were on our way to learning how to drive on German roads. We were soon to experience, from the driver's seat, the famous *autobahn* and encounter highly skilled but ferociously fast German drivers. There was specialization within their speedy impatience: sporty BMW drivers would weave and whiz in and out of city traffic, whereas the car suddenly appearing behind you on the highway, flashing its headlights in the fast lane, was more likely to be a Mercedes-Benz.

~!~

PLAYING CHICKEN

Not knowing the German word for "egg." Forgivable. Not knowing how to eat an egg. Pathetic.

When soft-boiled eggs are served in European breakfast rooms, they're propped pointed-end-up in darling little egg holders. These porcelain cups are delicately painted and shaped like an hourglass, with a thin neck in the middle and a solid base.

Charming. But how to attack the egg? With your knife? With a fork or spoon? Should you grab one, chase it around your plate, and peel it like a hard-boiled egg? Then what? Somehow coax it back into the little cup? Could get messy.

We had arrived in central Germany and were living in a hotel for several weeks, waiting for permanent housing. The learning curve was steep. For example, how do you negotiate breakfast gracefully?

Wait. Stall. If this is your first time approaching a soft-boiled egg in a foreign country, dawdle and watch your neighbors. The Book of Proverbs tells us that, "even a fool, when he is silent, is thought to be wise." If we don't say or do anything, we won't appear too gauche. We watch and wait.

Eventually, we learned that the knife was the correct implement for beginning the task. You saw across the narrow top of the egg, lift it off, and set it aside. Now take the tiny paddle. It's square-bowled like a snow shovel the size of a free ice-cream-tasting spoon. Now don't just sprinkle the little guy with salt and pepper. Pierce the white, and place a dab of butter into the golden, molten middle. *Guten appetit!*

Wunderbar. Now you know how to consume these individual servings of three-minute protein. Savor them as a filling boost with your *brötchen* or croissant. If you can find them.

Sometimes soft-boiled eggs are offered by the waitress. Sometimes they're set on the sideboard. On a business trip in Europe, I noticed everyone around me eating eggs. Little egg cups and mini spoons were lined up next to a covered basket at the buffet. The basket had a wicker base with a gingham liner gathered and tied at the top. It seemed like a lot of fuss to tie and untie a ribbon between each diner's serving, but I set about the task. Once opened, the fabric square revealed only a plastic lid. If I'd lifted the lid off the basket instead of dismantling the decorative cover, I'd have seen a nest full of eggs. *Was anyone watching me do that?*

On a vacation, we noticed an arrangement of egg cups and spoons on the community breakfast table. No basket of eggs. Neither were we offered any by the server who brought us coffee and cocoa.

Maybe the soft-boiled eggs were under the pink, quilted-chicken centerpiece. Like a tea cozy. I lifted the whole thing. Nothing incubating under there. No opening at the top. I craned my neck to see if someone else would reveal the solution to the puzzle. No one did. My watch-and-wait strategy wasn't working. I sipped my hot chocolate slowly. By now it was 9:30, and there was no one left to watch. Should we track down a server and demand our free eggs? Maybe we were too late for eggs. I couldn't take the risk. It was too early in the morning to face that kind of rejection.

"You ask," I goaded my spouse.

The waitress reached toward one side of the pink hen and lifted a quilted wing to procure a warm, white egg still in its shell. And then another. "The eggs are inside the chicken," she informed us. Naturally. That's where eggs come from. *I knew that.*

◦⫯◦

WHERE'S THE KITCHEN?

When my brother was three years old, Mother took him to Paris to visit her French family. He entered our grandmother's tiny seventh-floor flat, took a quick survey of its three tiny rooms, and immediately inquired, "Where's the refrigerator?" There was no such thing. Embarrassed, Mother shushed him and pointed to the windowsill, where a package of butter and a small bottle of cream sat cooling on the ledge outside.

Thirty years later, I entered the apartment we had just rented in Germany and asked, "Which room's the kitchen?"

All the rooms looked alike in the unoccupied flat. Empty cubicles were painted a dull white and ready to be wallpapered. Solid-wood doors with lever handles and keyholes closed off spaces, even the living, dining, and kitchen areas. Wires dangled from the center of each ceiling where light fixtures wanted to be installed. No curtains anywhere.

The kitchen was barely distinguishable from the bedrooms except in two respects: It was a bit narrower, and a few things were sticking out of the wall: a high-voltage plug and a couple of capped pipes. There were no built-in cabinets, no closets, and certainly no appliances. When completely outfitted, the kitchen would look like a dollhouse. The refrigerator would be four feet tall, freezer compartment included. No excuse for not cleaning on top of this fridge; it was easy enough to see and reach. The stovetop would have flat, metal *platten* instead of open coils that boiled-over soup could spill through. There would be a single sink with the hot and cold water coming out of separate spigots. Do your own temperature mixing.

Some homemakers considered themselves lucky to have automatic dishwashers. Made by companies such as Bosch or Siemens, the appliances were energy-efficient but, like their clothes washers, took an eternity to run a load. I thought I wanted a dishwasher until I saw the chalky *kalk* deposits that built up from the hard water. Germans make some of the world's most famous crystal, but it requires extra attention to keep it sparkling. Various commercial products offered relief, but the best remedy was a rinse with strong vinegar (28 percent acid). Don't splash that in your eye, my medically alert father warned. You'll burn your cornea.

When winter approaches, residents grow to appreciate the doors that divide living areas. Radiators heat every room but not the halls and stairwells, so it's important to be able to close them off. Residents of modern homes are lucky to find flat, rectangular radiators under the window ledges rather than the old, ribbed type that collect dust on a hundred curved and angled surfaces.

The houses are boxy structures; even the interior walls are made of thick concrete blocks. The windows are double-glazed and have heavy, dark, wood frames with a two-way feature that lets them hang from side hinges to open wide or fasten at the bottom to tilt slightly away from the wall and allow some ventilation at the top. Nobody's gonna huff 'n' puff 'n' blow this house down. Enhancing energy efficiency and privacy are door and window *rolladens* that glide shut when the sun sets, protecting heat and seclusion.

In Holland, it was said, the lace curtains stayed open long after sunset. The Dutch, we were told, were proud to have passersby see their living rooms full of family treasures and happy guests. In our new place, there was a lot of work to be done before privacy or entertaining could be enjoyed.

"I've moved fifteen times, but this is the worst," said a retired sergeant turned government contractor. "I thought moving into army quarters was bad, but I wasn't prepared for this business of outfitting your own kitchen and buying wardrobes." The novice house hunter may overlook an apartment's absence of closets but, upon moving in, will realize the lack immediately.

"It's a mess," the man said. An expensive mess, when the deutschmark-to-dollar ratio dipped below two-to-one.

Our search for the things that make a house a home took my husband and me to places called Bauhaus, Massa, and Wertkauf. Pen and pad in hand, we measured in centimeters while thinking in inches.

Like many Americans, we opted for the less-expensive, do-it-yourself wardrobes and cabinets. We planned to use them for a couple of years and sell them before leaving, but in no case would we ship them to the States where a wonderland of extra, little rooms known as closets would render them superfluous.

Most of these *schranks*, cheap or expensive, were outfitted with lock and key. Very old-world. The arrangement becomes a nuisance because the key is needed to latch the cabinet door whether you wish to lock it or not. Half the time, the key falls to the floor when you open the closet. Why can't they use simple magnetic clasps?

The cabinets we purchased and installed were streamlined and shallow. Extraneous dishes must be stacked or stored downstairs in the *keller*. A two-piece kitchen *schrank* was on sale, preassembled, and John was able to enlist a colleague with a van to help him pick it up. Both parts were rectangular, but they had different dimensions. The top was taller but narrower. The guys were confident they could haul both pieces at once if they arranged them right. They loaded the base first, then tried to set the top upside-down over that. No, too wide. Maybe lay the base on its back and wedge the top in at an angle? Unload, reload. No, too tall. How about the other way around: start with the top section and balance the base on it? Still no. Any configuration they tried resulted in a near-fit. It was off by a quarter of an inch. A few stubborn millimeters. No use. After forty minutes of hoisting and hefting up and down, in and out, the men decided they'd have to make two trips to our apartment to get the cabinet home. Driving there and back twice would have taken less time than they'd spent trying to solve an unworkable puzzle. Another friend, Henry, hearing the story later, got a good laugh out of it. "I would have done exactly the same thing," he said.

The other cabinets and chests of drawers came unassembled in large, flat cartons with German directions and a rough sketch with the occasional detail omitted. Details like: hammer in the shelf supports and drawer runners before assembling the exterior walls; use the screws here, the bolts there, and save the washers for use with the larger bolts. Sitting on the living room floor, we misinterpreted the line drawings, applying screwdriver and wrench, doing and undoing, getting a piece almost done before we figured out some part was upside down or backward or fastened with the wrong hardware.

Similar projects can be ordered from well known catalog companies in the United States. They might be approximately equal in quality and similarly explicit in their directions (or not). But at least they don't have the temerity to mark the cartons with, *"Selber bauen macht Spaß."* Building it yourself can be fun.

ᕤ❢ᕥ

QUIET ZONE

The cabinets had to be assembled before we could unpack everything, so we set about that task right after lunch, banging boards and pounding pegs into *schrank* parts according to the Ikea instructions.

Pretty soon there was a knock on the door. A young woman with short, dark hair asked if we could "stop that bumping."

"I'm sorry. We won't usually be this noisy. We just moved in, and we're getting some work done."

"We have quiet hours."

Ruhezeit was observed from 1 to 3 in the afternoon, starting again at 10 o'clock nightly, and all day on Sunday. Not many Germans were active churchgoers, but they did faithfully observe the Sabbath Day.

We later learned that a forty deutschmark fine could be imposed on people who blatantly defied the ban, and we heard of a guy who paid the price for polishing his sports car's wheels in front of his rented house one unusually sunny Sunday. The rules were observed rather stringently in rural communities. A big-city dweller explained that it was harder to enforce regulations in a metropolis, where the population tended to be more unruly.

"I can see where quiet hours might be nice, especially with so many people living in apartments," my mother commented on her next cassette-tape-letter. "I remember when your father and I had been married a couple of years, we lived in that depressing little place with the blue walls in Washington, D.C., and the woman upstairs used to vacuum every morning. Now, I'm clean, but I've never heard of anyone vacuuming the entire apartment every day."

"Your father was in pharmacy college then, and he was trying to study and work at the same time. I used to take your brother for walks if he got fussy, so he wouldn't disturb his dad. And then there was this female up there making all that racket."

"One day, her vacuum cleaner quit working, and she came knocking on our door to see if I could help. I asked her if she had changed the bag recently, and she gave me a blank look," Mother recalled. "She had recently come from Germany, and she didn't know much about appliances. She didn't realize the machines had a bag inside that needed to be emptied now and then."

"*Zut!* I shouldn't have told her. Then one day, the thing would have exploded all the dust in her face, and we would have had some peace for a change."

Mother was not predisposed to give Germans the benefit of any doubt, given her experiences in France during World War II.

Our language teacher had told us not to be insulted if new neighbors didn't seem friendly. If they didn't come to your door to borrow the proverbial cup of sugar the first day they moved in.

"Many Germans never get to know the German families who live right next door to them," the teacher counseled. People of that generation took their time making acquaintances. They were formal and reserved.

Still, one hoped to get along with one's immediate neighbors, and offending Beatriz did not make for an auspicious beginning.

Some time later, she invited me down to her apartment for tea and explained that she was studying for nursing-school exams. I offered her a plate of Snickerdoodles, John's favorite cookies. How was I to know that my neighbors were Greenpeace vegetarians who shunned processed foods? That they regularly had friends over to sing the socialist anthem *Internationale*? That perhaps they were not thrilled to have neighbors affiliated with the American military?

We had noticed the huge "35" stickers plastered on their little red auto, including the windows and the hood. "Thirty-five hours are enough!" It was the slogan for a movement to reduce unemployment and improve quality of life by shortening everyone's workweek from forty to thirty-five hours. A sort of job-sharing plan.

The day we'd met had been a difficult day, Beatriz told me. She had been questioned by television news reporters that morning, and she and Dietmar were eyeing the television to see if she would be on the air. The interview followed a weeklong seminar she'd hoped would address the discrimination endured by Jews in Germany, and she had been willing to voice her opinions to the media.

"All week long, they talk about philosophy and theology," Beatriz complained. "They know nothing of the difficulties faced by Jewish people here today."

"Do you experience harassment?" I ventured.

Her dark eyes regarded me seriously.

"I am studying to be a nurse," she explained in her slow, careful English. "Every day I go to Mannheim. I have something on my car – how do you say? [A bumper sticker.]. It says, 'I love Israel.' In the evening, I find swastikas painted on the sticker and on the car doors, and threatening words written."

My mother was held in a detention camp when Germans occupied France, I told Beatriz. She'd had serious misgivings about my coming to this country, all these years after the war. "She was afraid there were still Nazis in Germany."

"Your mother is right," Beatriz responded, her eyes flashing. "And there are many, even here in this town. Every day now, I have to check [for a bomb] under my car, because I am afraid."

Whenever they had a holiday, she and her husband would visit Israel, where she could soothe her psoriasis in the slick Dead Sea mud. The couple felt comfortable there and instantly welcomed, friendly with everyone. They had occasionally met Americans in Israel, "the rich ones" who were there to take the skin cure.

That evening our landlady stopped by unannounced to bring us a plate of sweet *zwetschgenkuchen* and to thank us for being so quiet, for not slamming shut the *rolladens* when we came home late at night the way the previous renters had done. Whether she was more concerned about noise or about saving her property from wear and tear, I wasn't sure. Was the cake offering for appreciation or was it an incentive? After she left, I pulled gently on the shutters' straps, easing them down to the granite windowsills.

Quiet hours.

᠊᠊I᠊᠊

EVERYTHING YOU NEED AND MORE

Shoes are squashed, leather chairs indented, vacuum hoses flattened, rugs curled, clothes rumpled after being shipped around the world to your next home. Most things will straighten themselves out, conforming to their original shapes. Just now, though, they are wizened impressions of their former selves, sleepy-looking after a three-month hibernation. They resemble tired children, awakened from hours of motionless slumber, their faces puffed and creased by the folds in their pillows.

Familiar objects peek out from a thousand shreds of packing paper to bring a festive feeling to a family settling in and reclaiming their household goods.

Trees die for this. To move a million Americans' tacky treasures from one military base to another. Every year, entire forests sacrifice their glorious, irreplaceable lives. Cheap quilted padding mounts in linty piles that are taller than the cartons they came out of. Paper rises up in weightless mountains in every room where boxes are being unpacked. Children relish playing in piles of the stuff. It scatters like autumn leaves when they run and jump, howling and giggling, to the exasperation of Mom, who is exhausted enough without the energetic antics. The excelsior entertains the tiny ones, but the contents are of utmost importance to the older children who have waited months for their books, toys, and games. They scramble from one carton to another searching for prized objects, because packers have a sense of humor, and a box marked "toys" may contain linens with one stuffed bunny on the top. A child's favorite fashion doll or a teenager's newest sweater could be anywhere.

Each crinkly piece of wrapping must be loosened and fingered to ensure that small objects are not discarded with the paper and cardboard. This is an easy way to lose a baby spoon, the lid to the sugar bowl, or the detachable legs of a coffee table with Kodak photos decoupaged on it.

"Shoes, shoes, shoes," a box is labeled. It does indeed contain footwear: what a packer must have deemed an indecent number of leather knee boots, ballet slippers, loafers, high heels, and moccasins. One big carton is full of stuff from bathroom cabinets. It's marked "spices and odds and ends" but turns out to be feminine hygiene products.

Somewhere among the mess are all the items needed. And more. Too much more. The Mother's Day plate, the plaster impression of Junior's hand, Granddad's chess set. Things the owners have largely forgotten they owned but, ninety days earlier, were sure they couldn't live without.

⸮!⸮

HEARTBROKEN TEENS

Half a dozen men were moving to Heidelberg to work for a government contractor. Half a dozen supportive wives were unpacking and settling into homes overseas. Half a dozen adolescents were moping.

Ermina had happily relocated as a child. Enjoyed grade school in Stuttgart. Back in Columbus, like a resilient "army brat," she'd readjusted to middle school in America. After her freshman year of high school, Dad had expected enthusiasm when he announced the family would be returning to Deutschland, a place they had all loved. This time, Ermina dug in her heels and had to be dragged overseas. She was leaving behind a position on the gymnastics team in addition to a coveted spot on the junior varsity cheerleading squad. And a steady boyfriend.

In a beautiful location in the Neckar River Valley, Ermina lay around the house all summer, writing long, daily letters to David. He was busy with football camp and a summer job, but he wrote her every week or so saying, yes, he still missed her, loved her. They'd have talked every day, but the telephone had a meter, and Dad would come home each evening and take a reading of units used. He'd grouse about the phone bill if he saw too much of an increase from one day to the next. A bill could easily amount to $200 well before end-of-month invoicing, and some parents were known to put lockboxes on their phones.

The humid summer days dragged by. School in the fall would bring welcome diversion but also the trial of meeting new people, trying to make friends, and figuring out teachers with unknown reputations.

We were at her parents' house, sitting down to juicy pork steaks cooked over an outdoor grill one evening in August, when Ermina came shrieking through the front door.

"I made cheerleader!" she announced with full yell-leader exuberance. "Varsity squad!" School had started that week, and things were looking up.

In the States, tryouts are typically held in the spring to allow new cheerleaders a chance to perfect their skills at summer camps. In the Department of Defense system, there were so many summertime reassignments, it made sense to hold team auditions at the beginning of the school year. This arrangement suited Ermina just fine, since her gymnastic talents were appreciated as much or more at this school as they had been stateside.

In September, she was happily leading cheers at pep rallies and football games. When October rolled around, a senior with a letter sweater and his name on the honor roll asked her to go to the homecoming dance with him. She said yes and pulled out the aqua gown she had worn to the prom with David in Columbus the previous spring. At the last minute, just as Steve was due to ring the doorbell, Ermina noticed the framed five-by-seven photo hanging in the entry hall, and she tossed it into a drawer. She was not concerned that it showed her with another boy. The problem was that she was wearing the same aqua dress.

She was sleeping late the next morning, half dreaming, half remembering the fun and friendship of the double date, when her mom knocked on the bedroom door.

"You have a letter from David. This is the third one in two weeks."

Why wasn't Ermina writing anymore, he asked. It had been a month since he'd heard from her. The tone of his letter was hurt, maybe a little upset, but the last line was optimistic.

"I haven't forgotten you, even if you are busy with new friends," David wrote. "I'm waiting for you to come back, and I know we're still going to get married someday."

❧ ⌘ ❧

THE MATTERHORN

After a three-year absence, Louvenia and Denton were back in Germany, happily shopping along a brick-paved pedestrian zone in their favorite village on the Neckar River. During Denton's tour of duty as an army officer, he and Louvenia had found it pleasant to sit and enjoy a coffee at a familiar street café. Better yet, an ice cream at her preferred shop. European ice cream parlors had elaborate menus of choices, laminated with enticing color photos.

One hot, humid day several years earlier, Louvenia had skipped lunch and thought she would indulge a bit after work. What looked good to her on that summer afternoon was a coupe called the Matterhorn. It was a large glass dish that was filled to the top and beyond with twelve colorful scoops of ice cream in different flavors and garnished with fruit, chocolate sauce, whipped cream, and a waffle cookie. The sort of mountainous treat that might be served with multiple spoons and shared around the table. Yum, that was delicious. But she still had an appetite. Why, she believed she'd have another right now!

Louvenia had what the French might call *du monde au balcon*, a rather crowded balcony. She was built like an inverted Bobo doll: big on top and tiny at the bottom.

Except that she didn't bounce back up very well. Standing at four-foot-eleven, she wore 48DD bras and size 3½ shoes. This was not a formula for stability. She could trip over a crack in the sidewalk. And she regularly did so.

Her face was round, her hair severely cropped and bleached platinum. Typically, she wore loose, stretchy sweaters since they accommodated her ample bosom. Working at the busy Heidelberg post exchange, she sometimes had to park down the street and around the corner. Past a restaurant that catered to Americans. Past low-rent housing. Past the place where hookers lingered to attract off-duty soldiers. Walking back to her car one evening after working a late shift, she was apprehended by *polizei* who mistook her for a street walker.

Women who are overly endowed get all sorts of unwelcomed attention. They also know the discomforts of bra straps cutting deep into their shoulders and the weight that makes vigorous exercise ill advised. I know several women who've had breast-reduction surgery, one of them so she could be more comfortable horseback riding. Lindsay, whose husband worked for Denton, thought this was what the boss's wife needed: a surgical solution. Louvenia was skeptical: "My husband likes them just the way they are," she informed Lindsay in her southern drawl.

"Really?" Lindsay's build was the opposite of Louvenia's. She was almost too thin, possibly because she was on a liquid diet – all alcohol – and she had perky little breasts under her favorite dusty-rose sweater. Lindsay was talkative to start with, and wine further loosened her tongue. She couldn't believe Louvenia's reaction to her helpful suggestion. "Well, my husband hates big titties," Lindsay exclaimed. Right to Louvenia's face. Repeatedly.

Ironically, for someone who might appear well equipped to nurse a baby, Louvenia was unable to bear children. Eventually, she and her husband adopted a son, but Denton never seemed as interested in fathering as she was in mothering. Once, when he was a tyke, Timmie was asked what he and his dad did on the Fourth of July. "Drink beer, piss on the fire, and howl at the moon," he declared.

The child was not interested in education. Eventually, he dropped out and became the unwed father of a local girl's baby. Her parents were less than thrilled with the situation and sought to cut off contact with the teenaged American boy. Louvenia was crushed to think she might not get to have a relationship with that baby. Maybe she wanted a second chance to help a child turn out right. Maybe she just loved babies.

As a German friend once told us, *"Kleine Kinder, kleine Sorgen; große Kinder, große Sorgen."* Small children, small problems; big kids, big problems.

Denton had been glad for a chance to return to Germany, this time as a government contractor. On their first available weekend, he and Louvenia returned to the quaint cobblestone street in the little town they loved. Who says you can't go back? The atmosphere seemed the same as it had been. Fruit stands outside small groceries. The woodsy smell of leather drifting from the same cobbler's doorway. Stylish displays in dress-shop windows. Ah, there was that dessert place they'd liked so well. The moment they entered, a commotion erupted behind the counter. *"Das ist sie! Das ist sie!"* The veteran waitress exclaimed to her newer colleague, *"Die Amerikanerin die zwei Matterhörner gegessen hat."* There she is! That's the one! The American who ate two Matterhorns.

A HAPPIER CAMPER

The radiators were shut off during the day, and the housekeepers would fling open the windows to air the place, so I'd sit freezing in the hotel room, wearing multiple layers of clothing. John was at work all day, and I was at loose ends. There was no daytime television except a Channel 3 signal pattern with a male voice repeating, *"Süddeutsche Rundfunk."* If I tried to use the telephone, a metallic female voice would invariably inform me, *"Kein Anschluß unter dieser Nummer."*

I would go out and walk the cobblestone pedestrian zone with its carefully curated shop window displays. But I hesitated to go into a store lest someone try to communicate with me.

The winter weather was cold and dreary, and I was lonely and homesick. Gray skies contributed to my glum outlook.

The clouds in Arizona were fluffy cumulus or striated cirrus. In late summer, they'd form tall cumulonimbus columns behind the mountains and develop into a dark, threatening gray. They were dynamic, happy clouds blowing in the wind and constantly changing shape.

In central Germany, the cloud cover was most often a solid, pale gray. No variation in color or texture. Little to indicate they were clouds, even. Just a static, colorless glare. They didn't look like individual clouds. That was simply the color of the sky. Sometimes I yearned to reach up and claw at it. I wanted to see if I could rip off the dismal shroud and find out if there was blue sky somewhere above it.

Then we got housing and a car, and I found a job (or it found me), and the world began to look brighter.

Mine was the loveliest commute in the world. Half an hour of gorgeous old-world charm, complete with thirteenth-century castle ruins. Twice a day, my route took me past forests, fields, and vineyards. Through hillside villages of red-tiled roofs and overstuffed boxes of geraniums bursting out on all the balconies. The flowers were a variety I hadn't seen in America, hanging geraniums that spilled, vinelike, out of apartment windows.

Suddenly, like Allan Sherman's summertime letter writer, I was a happier camper now.

On the weekends, we could visit the farmers' market, then go hike in the woods, where rich greens and browns would warm my senses. Near our flat was a shaded path along a golf course, where John would jog, and I'd ride the red Schwinn bike he'd given me the first Christmas after we were married.

Or we'd take a drive across farmlands that formed a patchwork of green and gold in every shade and pattern. Nowhere had I seen so much lush, intense vegetation. Where did it come from? It came from the sky. Gray sky was the price to be paid for all this green land.

If Arizona were rendered with watercolor, the German landscape would be done in rich oil paint. The only type of agriculture I had known consisted of citrus orchards and cottonfields. In my new home, farmers were growing copious amounts and varieties of foods. Long, neat rows of plump cabbages. Beets whose blood red color coursed through veins in their rumpled leaves. Stalks of corn shorter than anything John knew from the Midwest. The occasional field of hops climbing vigorously up wires, attached to supports like wooden telephone poles. Potatoes and sugar beets bursting from the ground and bulging from truckloads. Farmers in bright-green tractors holding up modern traffic for a worthy cause.

Never before had we seen hay bales that were anything but rectangular blocks. Here were big, cylindrical spools. For months, John would pass pale yellow fields of stubble, dotted by these round bales that were taller than a grown man, and he'd wonder how heavy they were. Finally, one day he pulled over to the side of the road, stopped the car, and jogged to the nearest bale to see if he could roll it. He pushed, and it budged a little. Satisfied, he jumped back into the car before anyone had a chance to see or say anything.

We were lucky to be in this bucolic setting, where life felt authentic, partly because we could see where our food was coming from and the people and lifestyle that produced it.

If you're from Germany or Switzerland and spend all your days there, do you appreciate the treasure of your land? Do you constantly drink in the natural beauty and historic value that surround you? Or do you cease to notice it?

Apparently, many Europeans do care very much about their environment.

In the deep shadow cast by the Holocaust, I dare not claim that Germany has always shown a great respect for life. Its people do, however, demonstrate a will to preserve *quality* of life. Protection of energy resources and architecture and forests. A forward-looking community leader established an exotic forest in 1871 that cultivates 130 species including giant red sequoia trees. In a castle park grows an 85-foot Lebanon cedar someone planted in 1835 that visitors still admire today. There are shared outdoor spaces with generous walking zones and bicycle lanes. And ample vacation to appreciate these precious assets.

◦⫯◦

YOU'RE WITH THE ARMY NOW

STILL SECOND CLASS

A good way to get a bad ID card is to have your picture taken immediately after a transatlantic flight. When your face, clothing, and hair look tired. This is not like your passport, which no one ever sees. No, you'll be using this little document every day. And no, you can't wait until tomorrow, when your hair's washed, because this laminated card is your access to every product, place, and process in the military world on your overseas assignment.

With this piece of plastic-encased paper, you'll be able go to the PX, bowling alley, arts and crafts shop, rod-and-gun club, commissary, movie theater, and library. You can enter the concessions where Hummel and Lladro figurines, Swarovski crystal, nutcrackers, Wedgwood, and Christmas ornaments by Steinbach and Käthe Wohlfahrt are sold year-round. You can go to the Class VI Supply store and buy alcohol. You can get on base to apply for a dependent-status job.

Getting official identification is the first stop in the "in-processing process." It is at this point that you are introduced to that military maxim, "Hurry up and wait." You rush to your sponsor's office to wait for a letter of authorization from the spouse's hiring agency. You hurry to the ID card office before it closes for lunch. Then you join a waiting room where people are scrambling to pick out white plastic letters to spell their names on black felt signboards. Hurry up; there's a line forming behind you. Hold the sign under your chin. Flash! Wait for your photos to be developed. If your eyes were closed, they'll redo it. If you look buggy-eyed, they're OK with that. Your opinion doesn't matter. Wait for your data to be typeset. Wait for someone to call your name. Wait for the plastic coating to cool.

Now you have a U.S. Army Europe identification card. Proper protocol will be essential. Your ID card must be shown for admission to installations and exchanges. Usually. You can't predict exactly when. Some post exchanges check identification when patrons enter the premises. Others let anyone in but check for required documentation at the cash register. Still other shops assume you showed your card at the main gate, or you wouldn't have gotten that far. A military police officer wants to see your ID when it's buried at the bottom of your purse.

This card makes you a bona fide member of the community. You are now officially "a dependent." A government spouse never uses her own social security number. She can forget the nine-digit series she memorized while standing in line to register for college classes. Nobody cares about that now. Only his SSN counts. His number goes on her ID card. His name goes on her medical records. He applies for her leave and emergency travel orders. He will be called if the children misbehave at school.

In this jungle, the sponsor is king.

∽I∾

GROCERY SHOPPING IS SWEET AND SAVORED

Stay away from the commissary on Saturdays, people advised me. On Sundays and Mondays, the grocery store on base was closed. On Tuesday, the checkout lines were backed up past the chow mein noodles, beyond the potato chips and cereals, around the rolls of paper towels, and through the giant bags of dog food, all the way to the carrot and onion bins. Military couples would pile multiple shopping carts to heaping, particularly on payday. Sometimes a day before that, when they could float a check.

I quickly learned to keep tip money on hand and to take special note of where I'd parked my car. Bag boys were in a hurry. They received no wages, so customers were expected to compensate them for separating perishables, not squashing the bread, and carting everything out to your trunk. I always wanted to ask how much they'd charge to follow me home and tote the groceries up the stairs for me.

Shopping at army or air force outlets, rather than on the civilian economy, was worth the inconvenience of showing IDs, waiting in slowly moving lines, and navigating crowded parking lots because of the remarkable prices. You didn't worry about the day's dollar exchange rate, and you didn't pay sales tax. Selection might be limited or supplies unreliable, but you recognized the brands and could understand the labels.

An added delight for me was the privilege of buying wares at facilities I could never even enter in my childhood. Living in a gate city, it was difficult to get onto the army base, let alone go into a post exchange or commissary. We weren't typically permitted into the movie theaters, bowling alleys, golf courses, or swimming pools. So, whenever I showed my ID card to go shopping on base, I smirked to myself as I was avenging the position my father had so often been in. Lead civilian pharmacist in an army hospital with a revolving door of active-duty pharmacy officers who seemed to get younger every year, he could be asked to join an on-post bowling league one year and be barred the next. One season, the golf course was opened to civilians, so Dad bought clubs of his own. The year after that, civilians were no longer welcome. In a larger city, it might not have mattered, but in a remote community of 7,000 people with no entertainment outlets of its own, the barriers were a constant reminder of exclusion.

Now I was in.

And the prices were favorable, despite friends and relatives having claimed they were no big deal. Funny: they insisted the prices were little different in the military stores than they were "on the outside." Yet they always made the longer drive to shop on post rather than in town. Some were afraid to offer to buy anything for you, even something not available for ninety miles around, because "if we did that, we might lose our privileges." When I was entitled to those privileges, I took full advantage of them and wasn't embarrassed to admit it.

Direct price comparisons can be sometimes confounding, though. Name-brand wrapping paper could be more expensive than the Christmas present it was covering. There were no generics or house brands. "Where's the stuff that comes eight rolls to a package?" one customer grumbled. "This is when you wish you could just run down to Walmart."

"The PX prices on designer jeans are great," a woman commented, "but who needs designer jeans to go wash the car?"

Shortages of particular items were often a problem at overseas commissaries. A customer snatched four cans of black olives off the shelf.

"They've been out of these for months," she explained apologetically. "When you see something you need, grab it today, because it won't be there tomorrow." Perhaps she could have walked down a red-brick lane to some little neighborhood deli and gotten genuine kalamatas.

Some women would jump on the autobahn every Saturday looking for a better-stocked commissary. If their husbands asked for bacon, they'd go in search of it. If their children wanted to bake chocolate-chip cookies, it was their mission to find Nestle's semi-sweet morsels in the bright-yellow bag.

Not I. If the Heidelberg stock was missing broccoli, we shopped in town or did without it. That might mean months of making pizza without mushrooms or substituting old-fashioned scouring powder for liquid Soft Scrub.

However, I did make a point of stopping at a big, out-of-town exchange once. On our way back from a Mercedes-Benz factory tour near Stuttgart, we passed Robinson Barracks, home of the largest PX in Europe. I couldn't resist. Maybe they would have tailored men's shirts. My favorite shampoo. Pantyhose and CoverGirl makeup in the desired shades. I wouldn't have gone all the way from Heidelberg to Stuttgart for these things, but, since I was there, I appreciated the superior selection.

Getting in line with my little shopping basket, pleased with my few finds, I overheard a soldier stationed in Stuttgart complaining to his wife, "They never have anything here. Let's drive to Heidelberg and see what they've got."

᠀᠊I᠊᠍

NO CENTS IN PX SHOPPING

"**W**hat would it take to get pennies into these cash registers: an Act of Congress?" The man in the checkout line was grumbling because the PX cashier had rounded up his $19.98 tally to an even $20.

In fact, it was not an Act of Congress but an action of the Department of Defense that induced the overseas penny shortage. The Lincoln penny has been around since 1909, but in 1980 it was declared too heavy to ship abroad. It was simply not cost-effective.

America has periodically considered eliminating the use of the Lincoln Head one-cent coin for multiple reasons. Because it costs two cents to produce. Because the copper is more valuable for electricians than for bankers. And because you can't buy anything with a penny anymore. Not a gumball or a toy or a Tootsie Roll. The penny is only good for paying tax. And that doesn't need to be added at the cash register, as other countries demonstrate every day.

It's not as though Europeans don't pay sales tax; in Germany, it was already a whopping 14 percent when I lived there. The VAT was included in prices marked on products as they sat on store shelves. No surprises at the checkout counter. More convenient than choosing a package of tissues marked 49 cents that's actually going to cost you 52 cents.

No tax was added to the subtotal at AAFES outlets, either before or after the net price of a product was marked. In fact, if you were shopping at the gift concessions, there was likely to be a discount subtracted at the last minute, depending upon that day's dollar-to-deutschmark rate.

The so-called penny shortage was not a problem. The Army & Air Force Exchange Service simply rounded prices up or down, and, in the long run, customers probably didn't lose much if anything. Most customers didn't complain about the system. Totals were easy to compute, and there was less bulky change to carry, wearing out the linings of your pockets. We got used to it. In fact, it caused a rude shock for Americans returning to the States to remember that a $5 bill wouldn't cover a $4.98 purchase.

No disrespect intended, Honest Abe, but your coin is nearly worthless. Compare it to the delicate dime, lighter in weight and ten times as valuable. Why do we even keep you around? Tradition, suspicion, and sentimentality, I suppose. Besides, if we do away with you, what will become of all those penny-filled jugs serving as doorstoppers in our homes?

⸓⟊⸏

GATEWAY TO GERMAN

After my first Gateway class, I stopped by my husband's office and ran into Monica, an American who had lived in Kaiserslautern as a child and was bilingual. Maybe I could impress her with my new-found vocabulary.

She beat me to it.

"*Wo ist der Bahnhof?*" she asked me, quoting the opening line of the Gateway to German textbook.

"How did you know?" I was surprised and a little disappointed. Not to mention naïve.

"Everyone knows that." Monica laughed. "Everybody who comes over here takes Gateway, and they all come out quoting the same little dialogue."

It may have been trite and tired, but it was also tried and true. Like the right key to open a door, the army's language program, while very basic, was indeed a gateway.

I was rediscovering what I had learned when my French aunt visited us in Arizona. That the sounds and syllables we call foreign words, those memorized dialogues and stilted phrases, did open doors. And get directions. And purchase goods. And get money changed. And make dinner arrive at the table.

Some frustrated students claim to have spent countless hours studying a foreign tongue in high school only to discover that they cannot make themselves understood when they visit the target country. Would that be the case if I used my new language downtown? Necessity made me try. I greeted a waiter in a restaurant, ordered lunch, paid for it, and even told him to keep the change.

The sentences in the phrase book worked.

It had been like that when I'd put my French to a live test ten years earlier. I tried a sentence on my Aunt Muriel, and she responded. She knew what I meant, and she answered me, and I knew what she meant. Magic. Mother, overhearing, was pleasantly surprised. "I didn't know you spoke *français*," she said.

That had been a proud moment. That, more than any "A" on a report card, was a payoff for my years of effort.

Now it was time to work on a second secondary language.

When I was a college student (the first time around), I sometimes felt impatient with middle-aged adults who had returned to school. Perhaps their children had grown up, giving them a chance to pursue their own interests at last. Maybe they had retired from the service and were using veteran's benefits to finish a degree. In class, they thought out loud, asked too many questions, and had a lifetime of anecdotes to share. Much later, when I became a professor, I appreciated how vibrant and engaged the more-mature students were. How undertaking this new endeavor was admirable, even brave.

In the army's Gateway to German program, those older students were still there, still offering different perspectives. Students came to the class with unique backgrounds. They'd studied at various institutions with different books. Or not at all. They had different strong points and weaknesses and thought that too much time was being spent on the wrong chapters. For some, however, the ignorance took on a whole new dimension.

Gateway classes were plagued by these students who had learned many lessons in life but had never picked up proper classroom protocols. Like the man who sat with a puzzled expression on his face when the teacher requested complete sentences in response to sentence drills. "Would a German person answer with a complete sentence?" the student challenged her. Or the guy who was presented with a phrase he found slightly awkward. The textbook lesson featured examples using the verb *geben*, "to give," drawing upon the limited vocabulary we had covered up to that point. *"Geben Sie eine Antwort,"* the sentence read. "Give an answer." The student complained that the sentence sounded unnatural and wanted to know if it was worth memorizing. "I just can't imagine a situation when I would use it," he said.

The one who drove me crazy – made me want to run screaming from the room – was Mrs. Wort. She stumbled on each concept and word, even obvious cognates.

Everything had to be repeated for her though the rest of the class got it on the first pass. *Berg* versus *burg*. Shall we try that a few more times? *Burg* versus *berg*. One evening, she was so befuddled by the question, "*Sind Sie eine gute Mutter?*" that she literally sat in awkward silence for several excruciating minutes. "Are you a good mother?" The teacher imagined Mrs. Wort either didn't understand the question or didn't know how to formulate an answer in German. The painful truth turned out to be that her moral code would not allow her to give a self-evaluation on such a personal matter. She couldn't grasp that this was a class exercise, not an inquisition.

Unless you're some kind of child molester, say, Yes, I'm a good mother, and move on. Let the class move on. Please! Before I jump out of my skin.

Gateway teachers were not professional educators. Not exactly volunteers but not well paid either. They didn't know how to appropriately pace the lessons or what to do with intractable students. Some of the instructors were more dynamic than others.

"*Guten abend.* I have a surprise for you," Teacher announced toward the end of the course. "We have been invited to speak to a class at the *Volkshochschule.*" The adult night school in town.

Our instructor knew a woman from New Mexico who was teaching English to German adults and was inviting our class to visit hers. We were each supposed to address our counterparts with a few minutes of facts about our

57

home state. The Germans would, in turn, inform us about various parts of their land. We could address our hosts in English if we preferred. The Germans showed us up by speaking English. Overachievers. One extroverted young man introduced himself as follows: "Even though I come from Hamburg, I am not a hamburger." He was, of course, in the same way that a person from Frankfurt is a Frankfurter.

Hiding behind props, I brought picture books of the Grand Canyon and handmade Navajo dolls to show. The little cloth Indians sparked great interest and many questions.

How were relations between Anglos and Native Americans, our hosts wanted to know. They asked us why Indians lived on reservations, if we respected their holy grounds, and how we felt about government-funded education and other benefits for our indigenous peoples.

"Do they all drive large cars like American Black people?" They must have been watching too many movies.

How to respond? Should we tell them only favorable things about our country out of loyalty and to enhance our image? Or should we share our problems and admit that we have unresolved issues? Which was the higher calling: patriotism or honesty? Our little band of unofficial ambassadors answered spontaneously and candidly, more concerned with penetrating language barriers than with contrived public relations.

Sometimes, on our way to a Gateway class, if the weather was at all pleasant, we doffed our work clothes in favor of boots, scarves, and blue jeans, and we headed to the *fußgängerzone*. There, on the walking mall, as the shops were closing and pedestrians were scurrying about on last-minute errands, we made our way to a *schnellimbiss* and ordered a quick kiosk meal. Then, perched on benches or outdoor planters, we listened to the string music of *zigeuners,* as the Romani were then called, and shared the steaming contents of our warm paper containers. *Bratwurst mit brötchen* for John. Flaky cheese-and-ham croissant for me.

The early evening sky was calm above the murmur of passersby. And for those brief interludes between ending the workday and beginning a night class, we could relax a little. We were content. Even as it was happening, I knew these were the times I would cherish long after the tastes and smells and sounds had faded.

"This is the life," John said as he wadded up his empty paper bag and we headed for class. "This is what we came here for, isn't it?"

❦❦❦

ARMY SECRETARY

My job as a civil servant was to type electronic messages since the head secretary did not do them well. The documents required certain forms and a special IBM Selectric OCR typewriter ball. The optical character recognition font featured all straight lines. The messages had to be done on special pink-and-white paper and typed precisely according to the prescribed format, or the transmitting equipment would not read them. The department's hope was that I could quickly qualify for a security clearance and be good at typing messages.

"Mrs. G has a fit with them. We try not to send any to her," the warrant officer explained. "She's a great secretary, an excellent typist, and a nice lady, but she doesn't do message traffic."

I met the division chief's secretary my first morning on the job. She was not the stereotypical civil service clerk in polyester stretch pants and a cardigan that sagged in the front. Nor was she the cool, efficient, business-suited professional of the carpeted and wallpapered offices of private industry. And she certainly was not the mini-skirted blonde bombshell "sexetary."

A gray cape and a wet umbrella blew in through the doorway. Beneath them was a tiny, whitehaired figure clad in a wool suit and smoke-colored stockings. A stint overseas was to be a final, preretirement tour of duty for Mrs. G's civil servant husband. Like many civilians, they had decided, at the end of three years, that they were not finished sightseeing, so they extended their stay for two years. It wasn't poor planning or procrastination that made them run out of time. Rather, their list of must-sees had grown as they went along. Before leaving Europe, they saw Switzerland, Austria, France, Holland, Belgium, and Luxembourg. Those were beautiful, so they ventured further. Boats up and down the Danube and Rhine. Castle visits. Cog-train trips. Ski lifts. The Wine Road. The stinky Cheese Road. Champagne tours. The tedious *Meistertrunk*. A cruise in the Greek Isles. A road trip getting lost in Yugoslavia. Then the Dalmatian coast beckoned. She returned from each trip with photos artistically taken, not the usual blurry, overexposed snapshots, and she faithfully kept a diary of their travels.

Having been division secretary for four years, Mrs. G knew where to place "TO" addresses and "THRU" addresses on memos. She could explain which letters required "For the Commander" above the signature block and how wide the margins had to be. This was helpful, but I learned not to stop by her bright corner of the *kaserne* when I was in a hurry. She was keen to share highlights of what was going into that travel diary.

The post chaplain likely merited a page in that journal. He was a passenger on a tour the couple took to Rome. The Papal visit began inauspiciously when the tour guide booked inadequate sleeping berths on the train. The chaplain thought to intervene helpfully but ended up throwing his hands in the air and exclaiming, "Who the hell organized this damned mess?" Mrs. G's eyebrows must have shot up, because the minister quickly quieted down. "Things have changed in the ministry," the clergyman mumbled as he trotted back down the corridor.

"I was brought up to believe that you go to church every Sunday, no matter how bad the preacher's sermons are," Mrs. G said. "So, we always go." She didn't say whether this chaplain's sermons were good or bad.

No one ever heard Mrs. G swear, not even when Captain Ashley's third and fourth drafts drove her to the height of frustration. She wasn't opposed, however, to imparting a colorful bit of criticism now and then.

"You know that visiting instructor?" she confided one Monday morning. "He never takes his hat off, even at the dinner party we went to Saturday. I told him right to his face that, if he were my boy, I'd turn him over my knee. Besides, I heard him making a date with that little private who's the courier from Frankfurt. She's nothing but a slut."

The dear lady was mightily unhappy when the clerical department was required to participate for ten days in a word-processing survey. This was to be an initial step in justifying the acquisition of computer word processors for the unit, a step that I favored, and Mrs. G dreaded. The survey project began with an hour-long orientation during which procedures were explained in excruciating detail. Computer acquisition promised to trade a short-term increase in red tape for long-term efficiency. Every minute of the day had to be accounted for, every typed document accompanied by an additional form describing its length, format, and degree of repetitiveness. The bureaucratic requirement stretched to the limit our top secretary's well known patience. She pulled herself up to her full five-foot height, eyes snapping, permed hair bristling, lips pursed, voice crackling, and announced, "I think this whole project is a drag!"

All winter, Mrs. G kept a heater plugged into a transformer by her desk, and she continued to use it throughout most of the year. "I had knee surgery, and I can't take the cold," she explained, lifting her plaid skirt to show scarred, knobby knees. "I was telling Specialist Smith about all these operations I've had – she's about eighteen years old, you know – and she asked me how I can wear a bikini with so many surgery scars. Can you believe that? I told her I'm a grandmother and I don't wear bikinis."

Before her husband retired and they left Europe, traveling by sea for an added adventure, I went with her to Mannheim to buy something to entertain her en route. She thought an electronic game would be fun for passing time on the ship going home. With some difficulty, we found a German version of a dot-eating video character known as *PucMan*.

❦

BLACK IN AMERICA'S ARMY

My colleague Sergeant Williams caught me off guard when I told him a woman had called during lunch hour and asked for him. She hadn't left her name. The young sergeant asked me if the person was his wife.

"I don't know. She didn't say."

"Well, do she sound Black?"

In truth I thought the caller might have been his wife. Yes, in fact, she did "sound Black" or Southern, but, at the sergeant's direct question, I hesitated.

"I don't know," I laughed. A silly, nervous laugh. I was lying.

He knows! I said to myself. Some people speak with a type of African American vernacular and accent. He did and so did his wife, and he knew it. Many soldiers exhibited pronunciations and grammar traditionally associated with a particular region of the U.S. Sometimes it was easy to detect whether a person came from Texas or Boston or New Jersey. Sergeant Williams spoke like a Southerner. He wrote like someone with limited formal education.

In 1955, the question had been, Why Johnny Can't Read. Now I was asking why Johnny couldn't write. Black or white, officer or enlisted, all were handing their secretary yellow legal pads with handwritten drafts replete with spelling errors and run-on sentences. It was pointless to start typing the memo on an electric typewriter, original plus carbon copy, before editing it with pen on paper. Sometimes the meaning of a paragraph was so unclear, I couldn't restructure the sentences without running the risk of misinterpreting. I had to ask the writer for clarification before I could prepare a typed draft for him. One soldier wrote Calvary for cavalry, and when I commented on the error, he gave me a blank stare. A major insisted on writing a memorandum about *espirit* de corps. He wouldn't believe that the word, even in English, was spelled *esprit*. At least he hadn't written *esprit de corpse*.

The first time an army private gave me an electronic message to type, I wondered why it was all in the present tense: "All item to be ship must be label." New to this unit, I was inexperienced with message traffic. Maybe this division used some sort of code for the sake of brevity in transmitting electronic messages. I tiptoed down the hall to ask the chief about it. He laughed. "That's just the way he writes," he told me. "He writes like he talks. You just clean it up."

In the writer's dialect, there was no "s" on the end of a noun to indicate the plural. Verbs were not conjugated conventionally. When I was in grammar school, I had learned "sound-it-out" spelling. So, apparently, had this soldier. He grew up writing what he heard. He just wasn't hearing the same sounds I was.

***

That evening, A.F.N. aired *Guess Who's Coming to Dinner*. Somehow, I hadn't ever sat and watched the film in its entirety. It was worth staying up late to see Tracy, Hepburn, and Poitier. Introducing the movie, the Armed Forces Network announcer gave a synopsis and apologized for its racial theme and language. "Remember, this was 1967," he said.

An especially poignant scene in the film is the one in which Poitier tells his father that the thirty-year difference in their ages has given them dramatically different attitudes. He'll always love his father, he professes, "But you think of yourself as a colored man. I think of myself as a man."

Decades later, *Boyz n the Hood* advised against joining the military, stating, "Black man ain't got no place in the army." In the film, Laurence Fishburne speaks from the perspective of a veteran of the Vietnam War, a conflict that saw African Americans serving and dying at rates far above those of whites.

As an outsider, I had a more positive perspective. My observation was that the military could give servicemembers wide opportunities in life and career. Discipline, pride, and physical conditioning. Clothing, housing, and steady income. Free medical care and discounted groceries. Training and education. While on active-duty service, soldiers who were willing to go to school two nights a week could return home with a college degree, maybe even a master's in some broadly applicable subject area like business or public administration or information systems management. Red or yellow, black or white, they could rise in the ranks or work toward a civilian career with job experience and veterans' hiring preferences. A step up.

Sergeant Williams began taking University of Maryland courses. I'd like to believe his experiences in the army ultimately improved his prospects.

~I~

THE SECRET

Today I am a woman. I will no longer be sent out of the room when secrets are shared. Big people won't whisper behind my back. I can read anything on any shelf.

April 22nd was my rite of passage. I had a Secret. That morning, I walked a little prouder. That day, I felt a little uncertain about how to conduct myself under my new status. Before, I had been told to leave the meeting so military personnel could discuss tantalizing topics of international import. Invariably, there had been tacked to my desk a red-and-black sign: "I do not have a security clearance."

Now, I could ceremoniously tear down that sign. Now, I was a full-fledged civil servant. Did I walk taller? Did I look more mature today? Starting today, I could file confidential papers and type not only messages but secret messages. Now, I discovered the responsibilities that went with access to The Secret. After applying for the higher security clearance, I read about loyalty and treason, about locking safes, and remembering not to reproduce classified documents, about distributing secrets strictly to employees having a genuine need to know. I was shown videos warning against telling civilian neighbors our travel plans and detailing the sobering fate of government spies.

Yearning to understand the true meaning of military life, I was excited to open and read a real Secret. To enter the secure vault and log out a file, to remove it from its folder, to scan its red-bordered cover sheet for the classified markings. To read it all the way through all by myself.

It was surprisingly unenlightening. I was unable to discern what was so special about this topic that everyone protected it and gloated over it. The first confidential document I had to type, using carbon paper that would be shredded and a ribbon that would be burned, contained a confusing array of numbers and letters used to identify communications security updates. That was it.

The Secret was not that fun or exciting after all. It didn't feel like a privilege or something worth celebrating or confiding to your best friend. That evening, I went home slightly disappointed in a rite of passage for which I had waited so long.

¤|¤

HE MAKETH THE SUN TO SHINE
UPON THE RICH AND THE POOR

Time weighed heavily in the air; the hands of the big, round wall clock could barely drag themselves in their relentless circles beneath a crystal spattered from the last time the government office had been painted. With all the officers on government trips or vacations, the office was quiet with too little going on. Even with the windows open, the only breeze we were able to produce in our third-floor barracks was stimulated by an electric fan that had been circulating warm air since 7:30 a.m.

I thought I had dressed for summer, which had arrived suddenly after my heavenward pleading for an end to a dreary winter and a cool, noncommittal spring. Shunning the usual skirt and blazer, I had opted for a cotton dress on this day. But my nylon slip and hosiery stuck to my damp skin all afternoon, and my limp hair was doing a better job of warming my neck in August than it had ever done in January.

An Arizonan through and through, I was unfamiliar with humidity, and it surprised me that, with all the moisture in the air, I could be so thirsty. Having little to occupy my mind allowed me to concentrate on my physical complaints. The empty hours dragged on, but I was so

71

restless and miserable, it would have been difficult to concentrate on a lengthy, involved project had there been one to do.

Finally, the day struggled to a close with the tired retreat of a faded U.S. flag, and I sank onto the sticky vinyl car seat. It was roasting hot, but I could endure anything for the minutes it would take to drive home. It was soothing to know that I would soon be able to strip off my damp garments and jump into a cool shower. And perhaps a second, quick shower at bedtime would render sleep possible in a land where nighttime lows were distressingly similar to daytime highs. Some measure of relief was in sight.

In Europe, the wealthy could keep comfortably warm all winter, but no one could stay cool in the summer. There was no air conditioning, and no one had evaporative coolers, which would have done little but add moisture to already humid air.

In the dimly lit apartment, *rolladens* drawn against the sun of an 18-hour day, I wanted to rip my clothes off, but moisture made the process more like unpeeling than undressing. As I tossed my clothing into the laundry, a sickening wave of dizziness swept over me. The longed-for shower didn't seem like such a good idea at the moment. I poured myself a glass of orange juice, popped the latest cassette-tape letter from my parents into the machine, and sat down. Trying to cool as much of myself as possible, as quickly as possible, I pulled away from the back of the chair, touching it only with my derriere and my shoulders. I took care not to touch any part of my body with any other part. Not to cross my legs or ankles or place my hand on my abdomen.

The tape-letter played, but I lost my concentration and drifted into a light sleep. When I awoke, it was 7 p.m. The gauges on the balcony read 36 degrees Celsius (97 degrees Fahrenheit) and 60 percent humidity.

Months earlier, in the depth of winter, colleagues had predicted this heat wave. "You'll see." It was meant as a threat, but through my three layers of woolens, it sounded like a promise. Back then, I'd sworn not to utter a peep about the heat if only the ground would thaw. So not once, throughout that steamy summer day, did I ever say, "I wish it weren't so hot." That was the worst part of the whole muggy experience. Not the heat or the thirst, not the dizzy spell or sleepless nights, but that silent restraint.

~!~

LOQUACIOUS LINDSAY

Access to the post hospital was a benefit that civilians could enjoy in the overseas setting. If you couldn't get in to see a military doctor quickly, though, you might consult a German physician. Lindsay did that and never got over the trauma of it. Going in for a general physical exam, she was required to undress as she was accustomed to. She was not given a gown, sheet, or towel, a situation she was unaccustomed to.

"I just sat there naked on that examining table," she cried out when she told us about it at the next happy hour. In her high-pitched Texas drawl, she told the story over and over. The more inebriated she became, the more she elaborated on her shame.

"Just buck-ass naked. I even had to cross the hall from one examining room to another without a stitch of clothing. Buck-ass naked." She was always talkative and often loud, but not usually so explicit. Once, I met the captain who was her boss and asked if she was equally chatty at work. Oh, yes, he said. She talks away all the while she's typing 90 words per minute. She's kind of crazy, but she's energetic, speedy, upbeat, and a great typist. He wouldn't trade her for any other secretary on the base.

The happy hour turned into a light supper, then late-night imbibing. Lindsay had promised to go to the holiday bazaar with me the following morning. As the evening wore into morning, I asked periodically if she were still interested in going to the Christmas market. Oh yes, she'd be ready, she insisted. At 8 a.m. sharp.

She was. In the same tired curly hair, smudged makeup, and dusty-rose sweater that smelled of smoke and alcohol from the previous night. She did have integrity. Or at least grit.

CAJUN MAMA

Sergeant LeJeune sat at his metal desk wearing a camouflage uniform and shiny black boots. Shortly before lunchtime every day, he would pick up the receiver on the heavy black telephone and dial his home number to ask his wife what they were having for dinner. Then he'd proceed to tell her what kind of meat he wanted and to instruct the missus on how to prepare gravy from a roux made with real butter. Or maybe he'd settle for a simple dish that evening. Something like jambalaya.

LeJeune had grown up in Louisiana but, typical of third-generation offspring, he knew only a few words of his ancestors' native tongue. He liked practicing his *bonjour* and *au revoir* with me in his daily comings and goings, but that was about the extent of his fluency. Like many Québécois, his Cajun family considered themselves French. My Parisian mother might not have agreed.

When the sergeant got to reminiscing about his mawmaw's peculiarities, he would come ask me if my mother had similar ways. This was his effort to discern what was a family trait and what was cultural tradition. Most of the menus he described were unfamiliar to me, though the titles were French. The housekeeping procedures, however, had much in common.

"So, your mother is French," he might say. "Did you have to take your shoes off in the house?"

"*Mais oui,* of course." I was so well trained, I took my shoes off at other people's homes too, even when she wasn't there. "I want them to remove their shoes in my house, so you remove yours in theirs, whether they ask you to or not," Mother insisted. You'd better not have damp, sweaty feet either, as those left footprints "on my clean floors." My father got so exasperated with her standards that he threatened to hang vines from the ceilings so he could swing, Tarzan-like, from room to room without stepping on her shiny asphalt tile.

"Did you get in trouble for touching the walls?"

"Oh yes." Our walls were pure white. No pictures were hung anywhere, and you were never to put a hand on the walls or lean against them. Even big, blustery Uncle Homer yielded to my 96-pound mother. Homer was a retired town marshal; he still wore his black cop shoes and a button-down shirt with a pack of cigarettes tucked in the chest pocket or into a rolled-up sleeve. He'd enter the house wearing those shoes, and Mother would frown. When he leaned on the wall, she spoke up. He might backtalk a little, but he'd pretty much do as she said. She called him "a mess," but you knew they liked each other. On birthdays, they'd exchange greeting cards that ranged from naughty to raunchy. She was feisty, and he was gruff and irascible. He'd call a niece or nephew "Worthless," then take them out on his rounds in a big, white pickup truck while he investigated people who had applied for workmen's injury compensation but were doing construction projects in their back alleys. One of Homer's favorite family stories centered on my French mother's accent. She could pronounce the letter "H" but tended to do so in all the wrong places. One summer, while the extended family went camping, she went fishing with Homer in an old rowboat. Focused on pulling in a big rainbow trout, he neglected the navigation. Seeing the paddles slipping out of their oarlocks, she cried out, "'Omer, 'Omer, look out for your Hoars!" He was so overcome with laughter that the oars did indeed slide away across the lake.

Mother generally had things her way; in the twenty years she reared children in that house, the walls were never once painted. They never needed it. We didn't realize the ceilings had not been painted at all until my brother and I were playing in the bathtub, squirting sudsy water from a tube of Prell shampoo. Splat! It was gratifying to be the kid who made the water spurt all the way to the ceiling. Oops! A wet spot appeared up there on bare, textured drywall. Suddenly we quit giggling and began strategizing to keep our mother out of that room until the spot had time to dry.

"You couldn't lean your head back against the sofa (and it was not a couch; it was a sofa) because you might have grease on your hair that would stain the upholstery."

"Right."

"No birthday parties."

"Nope. It's just another day."

"To be observed strictly *en famille*."

So, I hadn't had party balloons. This deficit cost me when some silly playground game involved inflating balloons and taking turns sitting on them to make them pop. It seemed like an undignified practice to me, but the teacher insisted that I participate.

"But I don't know how to blow up balloons!"

"Oh, of course you do. You have birthday parties, don't you?"

"No. My mother doesn't believe in them."

Pause. "Oh."

The similarities between the sergeant's New Orleans grandmother and my Paris mother continued to amuse him. There had been no other French children at my school, but, years later, it was comforting to learn that, somewhere in the country, someone else had stood out from the crowd in curious little ways.

One Monday morning, Sgt. LeJeune came into the office so eager he was about to burst. He had remembered something on Friday night and been saving it all weekend.

"We couldn't sit on the bed," he exclaimed. "I'll bet you didn't have that rule."

"Are you kidding? Of course not. We were never allowed to sit on the bed once it was made." It had been ages since I'd thought about that. My bedspread was a frilly, snow-white organza with tiny, pastel roses flocked here and there

79

on the quilted top and gathered skirt. No one was to sit on it. Ever.

That was one of many house rules that discouraged me from bringing friends home. On the rare occasions when I did, my classmates would naturally shun the desk chair and immediately plop themselves on that pristine bedspread in their faded jeans. Mother would pass my bedroom doorway and frown until I corrected my pals. If I didn't, she would whisk into the bedroom, fold back the spread, and ask my visitor to please sit on the exposed blanket instead. After she left the room, my girlfriend would give me a quizzical look. So, I rarely brought friends home. Which was probably the desired effect anyway.

HOLIDAY INN

Arabelle was tending to her thriving rose garden one afternoon when Mother greeted her across a fence, an oleander hedge, and a mulberry tree that periodically dropped nasty little fruits all over our car. "How are you? And how is Ed? I haven't seen him for a while." They were an older couple, and he had suffered a previous heart attack, so it was a natural question.

"He's got TDY again," Arabelle replied.

"Oh!" my mother replied. "I'm so sorry to hear that." That evening, she asked my father, our resident expert on all things medical: What's TDY, and what's the prognosis?

It was government talk for temporary duty in a different city. Some people wonder if the "Y" is for "yonder" as in "temporary duty over yonder," but the abbreviation for duty is "dy," so TDY is an extension of that. Why a four-letter word needs a two-letter abbreviation is another question.

When my husband got TDY, I was the one who felt ill. I hated to be alone overnight. Growing up, I was never alone; after I was married, I'd go stay with my parents during John's trips to Washington, D.C. or Maryland or San Francisco. In Germany, I had to be brave. Which to me meant abandoning the bedroom with its glass balcony door and sleeping in the bathtub because the bathroom had one small window and a heavy, locking door. Worse yet, being alone meant I couldn't call my mother from down the road to get rid of a lizard that had crept into the apartment, and I had to kill my own spiders.

John's return flight out of New York was scheduled to arrive early in the morning. It would be nice to have him home, but I was nervous about recognizing each of the *autobahn* intersections between our town and *Flughafen Frankfurt*. I got up at 5 a.m. and, in spite of the fog, my anxiety, and a plethora of road signs to decipher, I managed to find not only the airport but a parking garage as well.

In Hall B, downstairs outside the luggage claim, I checked the massive board listing international, incoming flights. TWA flight 740 had been expected at 6:30 when I arrived but as I watched, the digital read-out changed to 7:15. An hour. It figured: I was early; he was late.

A collective sigh arose from the crowd. There were many others awaiting the jet, most of them Americans. A man with a military haircut stood holding a bouquet of red rosebuds and a teddy bear. He caught me watching him and volunteered, "My wife and daughter are coming in today. I finally got quarters." Married housing.

Nearby, a quiet, young woman stood in a frilly pink dress and patent leather heels. Her hair was fine and blond and styled in neatly placed curls. She had a baby face, but she wore full makeup from ruby lips to darkly penciled eyes. How early had she gotten up to make a good impression on her man? Behind her, a boisterous family had clustered. The ringleader was a large woman in a polyester knit blouse with big, orange flowers on a black background. At her feet were a toddler in a stroller and a preschooler with his breakfast still on his face.

"I knew this would happen," the woman told her parents. "Didn't I tell you? That flight out of New York is always late. It comes from Las Vegas, and I'll betcha' it was late getting from Vegas to JFK. That's what happened."

"Billy, get over here, right now. Don't go wanderin' off. Stand over there by Grandma."

Luckily, I had brought my trusty paperback, so I headed upstairs to the rows of black vinyl seats to sit and read near the arrival gates. It was comfortable there, and I could catch John between the gate and the luggage conveyor belt. There was no display board with flight information there so, when the hour was almost up, I headed back downstairs to Hall B. The crowd was still there. The man with the flowers rubbed a finger absent-mindedly on the teddy bear's fur. The girl in the high heels shifted her weight from her right leg to her left. The woman in the synthetic print was talking about long lines at the commissary and complaining that it wasn't fair that they didn't carry her favorite brand of cigarettes.

Flight 740 was not yet marked *gelandet* in the left column of the digital board. It hadn't landed. There was nothing in the right column where the expected arrival time should have been. The description now read, "New York *über* Bonn/Köln." The flight had been rerouted due to the fog, and a half dozen others on the panel were being similarly updated.

A hundred people waited for updated arrival estimates. When it said 8:40 by John's flight, I headed back upstairs. The woman in polyester was explaining to no one in particular that, after the fog lifted, planes stopping in Cologne would have to be squeezed into existing landing schedules before they could fly back to Frankfurt. The baby in the stroller was crying as I rounded the corner. "Billy, I've told you five times to leave your little brother alone."

At 8:50, the estimated arrival changed to 10:15. The blond girl's curls were starting to fall. The rosebuds were beginning to open, and the romantic young man was dangling the teddy bear by its ear. I was halfway through my book.

The estimated arrival continued moving back in increments as it generally does, an hour at a time. This led us to suspect airline officials knew the truth all along but were afraid the crowd would turn ugly if a six-hour delay were honestly announced upfront. So, everyone waited in the airport, paying the equivalent of seven dollars for a bottle of water and four dollars an hour to park. They might have taken a streetcar downtown to have a proper lunch or do some shopping if they'd known the whole story.

By 12:50, the girl in the high heels had found a seat and was twisted sideways, resting her sagging curls on the faux-leather, the lacy dress now damp and wrinkled. The thirsty, red roses were limp. The large, floral woman was

84

complaining that it had taken her three months to get her baby into the well-baby clinic for his six-week checkup. Junior had barely fallen asleep on a wadded-up jacket by a pillar when Flight 740 finally landed, and his mother woke him up and dragged him to the gate where passengers were entering the terminal.

"That can't be our flight," said a short-haired, middle-aged woman in a professional-looking suit. She had been waiting for the same flight I was, but she was sure this was not it. The first group of incoming passengers consisted of small, dark-haired men in dull business suits. The next cluster featured too many pairs of pointy-toed suede boots, too many heavy coats, and too many people wearing winter hats.

"I don't think that's it, either," she whispered with a laugh.

Finally came a man carrying a tennis racket, a couple in khaki pants and polo shirts, an older guy in corduroy slacks and a windbreaker, and lots of folks in tennis shoes. And one middle-aged white guy in cowboy boots and hat (where did he put that thing during the long flight?).

"Does this look more like it?" I asked. She nodded.

The tired preschooler ran through the restraining bars to jump into Daddy's arms. Next to me, a couple began to hug, and a tired young woman graciously accepted a wilted bouquet. A girl in a frilly dress and high heels was lifted off the ground by a tall man with a crew cut.

John came out wearing an apologetic expression as passengers sometimes do when they know someone has been waiting for them a long time, though it's not their fault they're late. I gave him a big hug, and we headed for our next opportunity to stand in line: baggage and customs.

On the curb outside, I waited with the luggage while John went to get the car. A family from New York was rushing nervously in one direction and then another.

"I can't find the shuttle bus to our hotel," the mother said.

"I don't know why you brought so much luggage for a three-week trip," the father grumbled.

"Let's just take a taxi," the woman said, rushing in the wrong direction.

"Taxi?" I intervened and pointed behind her.

Thrilled to find a helpful soul, she latched onto me. "Holiday Inn?" she asked. "Holiday Inn?"

I could probably have found her ground transportation, but before I had a chance to open my mouth, she repeated, slowly and firmly, "Hol-i-day Inn!"

"Taxi?" I repeated. The woman leaned toward me, her face close to mine, and enunciated loudly this time, "HOL-I-DAY INN!" Before I could say another word, she went rushing off hysterically in the opposite direction, and I never knew what became of her.

∽ǃ∽

MATINEE IDLE

When John went on TDY, I had to fend for myself. With few acquaintances and too little courage to drive more than necessary, I faced limited options for occupying myself. No local language skills, so no TV to watch. It was easy to get lost in a sea of time. No noon phone call to punctuate the day. No evening arrival at the door to mark dinner hour. No disciplined bedtime since there would be no morning alarm.

The landlady's looping her wicker basket over the bars of her one-speed bicycle signaled the approach of a weekend. And that called for doing something a bit special.

I scanned the movie schedule, and the only title I recognized was Walt Disney's "One Hundred and One Dalmatians." The matinee. Good. I was relatively comfortable driving to the nearest army base and back in the daytime.

When I pulled in front of the theater, I almost lost my nerve. The line, backed halfway down the sidewalk between the theater and the chapel, was ninety percent children. The other adults were there as chauffeurs or chaperones. It was going to be noisy, and I was going to be out of place.

I knew grown men who enjoyed cartoons, but they watched Saturday morning TV programs or rented videos to watch in the privacy of their own dwellings. They didn't stand outside theaters in broad daylight, advertising the fact they had nothing better to do than watch a decades-old kids' show alone. If they went to kiddie shows, they had kids in tow. If only I had thought to borrow one.

Still, I'd be at loose ends if I went straight back home. So, I marched resolutely to the end of the ever-lengthening line and pulled out a library book, a habit that had quickly become my answer to the bureaucratic waiting game. The book happened to be an anthology of essays on the population explosion. As I stood among the mass of children, I was reading a *New York Times* piece about birth control.

When I reached the window, the ticket taker asked his standard, "How many?"

"One."

"One adult?"

"Yes, please."

"How many children?"

"None. Just one adult."

As I headed for the lobby, I heard a man's voice behind me say, "One adult ticket only, please." It was a twenty-year-old off-duty G.I. in dark glasses. He was wearing a red-and-white soccer jersey screen-printed with the number 18 and the word "Loverboy."

The national anthem played, the lights dimmed, and the animated flick began. It had been years – decades – since I'd watched or even thought about Cruella De Vil or the giant litters of spotted pups. Children in the audience cooed over the first fifteen puppies. So did I. The kids sneered audibly at the villainess. So did I. They cheered for the dogs in the snowy chase scene. So did I. When a puppy crawled under a blanket and tucked itself in, some in the youthful audience sighed contentedly. So did I. When the film ended and the house lights came on, all the kids and parents looked happy. So did the guy in the soccer shirt. You didn't have to be a TDY widow to need the company of strangers at a Saturday kids' cartoon. Apparently "Loverboys" got lonely too.

~I~

CAN THIS MARRIAGE BE SAVED?

Crash!

Through the concrete slab that served as our ceiling and the new neighbors' floor came the noise of something shattering. Something heavy made of metal and glass. Then a woman's voice reacting with a sound that could have been laughing or crying.

This was the first disruption from the couple moving in upstairs. It would not be the last. There were nights with hysteria. Maybe it was weeping. Were they fighting? It was hard to tell. *Should I intervene, ask her if she's OK?*

They were a beautiful couple in their twenties. Karen was bubbly, and Stan was polite and reserved. He called me ma'am when we met in the stairwell. He was in the military police. The landlord told me later, after the couple had moved out, that the heavy wooden frame around their bedroom door had been torn from the thick cement wall. With a smirk, the old man pantomimed his imagined scenario: She locks herself in the bedroom but he won't take "no" for an answer. Another crash!

Several months later, Karen told me Stan was being transferred to Hawaii. Hmmm. A chance for a fresh start in an idyllic location? Or a chance to let him move by himself so she could go home to Mama and rethink this relationship? I didn't ask.

The next time I saw her, Karen was excited. "Stan's getting an annulment. Now we can get married for real. In the Church."

***

An overseas tour of duty can make or break a marriage. You're far away from supportive family and friends. You might want to reinvent yourself the way teens sometimes do when they go away to college. You face new opportunities and temptations with no one who knows you around to reinforce your conscience.

"Remember who you are," my friend MaryJo always advised the young people she mentored. She cited the Bible verse in James that says, "For he is like a man who looks at his face in a mirror, and, after observing himself, goes away and immediately forgets what sort of person he is" (~James 1:23-24).

***

Sharon's job seemed to be sitting at her desk in her army boots and BDUs, dozing off until her head drooped and her neck jerked back upright. She was out too late last night. And the night before that. When she came home, she was disgusted to find that her roommates had not put away their dinner leftovers. It was one thing not to wash the dishes, she complained, but wasting food was inexcusable.

Sharon's roommate was not her spouse. Her husband was Stateside while she was at Army Headquarters –

Europe. They were both on active duty. They spoke somewhat regularly on the telephone, but a phone call from Europe cost $1 a minute, so you wanted to come up with something worth saying before you dialed. She was constantly trying, on those short and hurried conversations, to read between the phone lines to figure out how much he may have been fooling around on her.

He might well have wondered the same thing about her, as she seemed to have a string of boyfriends. A little private, also in battle dress uniform, stopped by her office one afternoon to flirt a little and remind her of their next date. After he left, she wondered aloud whether he was modestly endowed or whether she had gotten herself "stretched out" with the previous stud.

"He just feels like nothing," she overshared.

***

Veronique went to the Sorbonne to study French. She pursued an advanced degree and became an international-business translator. Then she met an army sergeant who was already twice divorced and paying child support in two directions. His favorite phrase was that the Marines were still looking for a few good men and he hoped they'd find them soon. He liked saying this to tweak her father, who had been a proud Leatherneck.

Their wedding featured military honors. A horse-drawn carriage took them from the post chapel to the reception hall. He wore dress blues. Her dress had the wide hoop skirt, deep ruffles, and puffed sleeves of a traditional southern ball gown. It was cherry red.

Two years later, she was an army wife living in Germany. Two years after that, she developed a huge crush on a smooth-talking colleague who conducted workshops on organizational behavior. He lived in a former castle overlooking the Rhine. She admired his rhetorical style, his Socratic questioning, his deep voice, his silver hair.

She'd go to his seminars and meet him for lunch. One weekend, her husband was on TDY, and Randy invited her to dinner at his small apartment in a big mansion. When he opened the door, he was in an old shirt, denim shorts, and sandals. She was in a brand-new black satin cocktail dress, red lipstick, and all new lingerie. She'd had her hair cut that afternoon especially for the occasion.

Randy apologized. She must have misunderstood his intentions.

"I'll *eff* your lights out," he said, "but not while you're married."

Veronique sat on Randy's sofa, her head on his shoulder, late into the night. Then he prepaid a taxi to drive her home, leaving her own car discreetly parked a couple of streets over.

By the time Veronique was divorced, Randy had married someone else. She vowed to remain single until he was once more available. Perhaps that might have happened, except that he died while she was waiting.

***

Patty married Bobby, a short and hairy man, because he asked her to. Not because she loved him, but because he loved her. Unlike the dashing graduate from her high school who begged her not to go through with the ceremony. "I think maybe *I* love you," he'd told her.

"But I *know* Bobby loves me," she replied. And promptly walked down the aisle and then flew to Kaiserslautern to live in married housing. Her new buddies were enlisted men and women who went bowling and drank beer.

The good things about Bobby were that he loved her and he was good in bed. "Don't underestimate a short man," Patty advised. "He can be everywhere all at once." The bad things were that he left hair all over the sheets. And that she didn't love him. And she was growing restless.

Eventually, Patty left him to go live with her parents and attend college. When she told him her decision, Bobby sat on the floor and cried.

At the university, she found a crowd of partiers including an attractive man she soon began an affair with. He was married, he told her, but he was only staying with his spouse until she'd finished paying his way through medical school.

Waiting in the cashier's line at a grocery store one day, Patty saw her lover's wife and three-year-old daughter. She recognized them from a photo she'd seen on the nightstand in his bedroom.

***

They met under a big canvas tent at a neighborhood *frühlingsfest*. On the long picnic tables were copious servings of beer and brats. Under the table, she was rubbing her bare leg against his. Before long they were on top of the table. The kitchen table.

She was miserable in her marriage, and he in his.

"Her husband is cold and unfeeling," he said. "His wife doesn't understand him," she said. Not the most original excuses, perhaps, but as Jeff Goldblum's *Big Chill* character observed, rationalizations are "more important than sex." Or maybe they lead to sex.

She moved out. He moved out. The lovers moved in together. But, at the risk of losing her portion of her husband's income, she refused to get a divorce. He wanted her to be free to marry him, but she would decline unless or until he "could shit quarters."

Back in the USA were ex-wives and ex-children left behind in that way some men have of moving on to a new wife and new offspring and forgetting their first family. Here in Europe were friends these guys hadn't met yet, new escapes, and new intoxications.

***

Erika was a bookmaker, she told us. She was young and professional looking. Impeccably dressed. Neat, short hair that was sprayed into place. Flawless skin.

John's response to her introduction was polite but slightly skeptical. You're probably not a gambling facilitator, he told her. I think you're probably a bookkeeper, he suggested.

When Erika and Werner invited us to their home for dinner, we knew they were a couple. We didn't know if they were married or not. They had different last names, but that didn't prove anything. With uncharacteristic discretion, we didn't ask. She made pizza topped with cauliflower. For the homemade crust, she substituted whole-wheat flour, and it came out tough and dry. She apologized profusely. We ate it and said it was fine.

Although they seemed determined to be our friends, we struggled to keep a conversation going with this painfully shy couple. She was an accountant and very quiet. He was a computer programmer and even quieter. They'd been together since their teenaged days, probably ten years earlier.

Germans get a lot of vacation time, so we decided that inquiring about their travels could be a productive line of inquiry. They showed us pictures from trips they'd taken to various European destinations in a long, red double-decker bus. They told us how the lower level was set up like a touring coach with large picture windows. The upper deck consisted of narrow bunks running horizontally, such that each passenger had to crawl into a long, narrow space with his head next to a little window at bedtime. This novel system made for economical and convenient travel. For those who could overcome their claustrophobia. We never tried it.

Seasons came and went, the four of us working full time and seeing each other only occasionally. It was usually a phone call from Erika that would initiate an evening out. One day, a square, cream-colored, linen-textured envelope arrived in the mail. We rarely received letters through the civilian system, relying largely on the Army Post Office, which was slow but cheap. Opening the formal announcement, we got our answer to the question of their relationship status.

No, Erika and Werner were not married.

Theirs was the most sedate wedding reception I've ever attended. There was no music. No dancing. Minimal drinking. A short toast made by one of the fathers. Surely there was a marzipan cake, but I don't recall it. John was out of town, and I sat in a stiff chair attempting German small talk with the groom's monolingual, monosyllabic aunts. The most memorable thing about that day was the bride's outfit, a nubby-silk skirted suit the color of bougainvillea with a black shell under the short, tailored jacket.

Yes, Erika and Werner were married.

The now-weds went on another Rotel-style trip that year. Then Werner announced he'd like to go on his own during a week when his wife was especially busy at work. The next holiday, he again proposed separate vacations. Shortly after that, Erika came upon a group photo from his hotel on wheels. The sort of picture everyone receives at the end of an ocean cruise. Standing by her husband was someone who looked familiar. She recalled that the woman and her travel companion had befriended Erika and Werner on a trip to the south of Spain. Now wasn't this curious? Werner was unaccompanied, and the other woman's partner was not in the picture either.

When Werner's dalliances were confronted and confirmed, and the new marriage fell apart, his parents defended him. They said Erika was cold and bossy. Always had been. He deserved a woman who would make him happy.

No, Erika and Werner were not married.

⌁I⌁

ANXIOUS IN THE ARMY

Private Penney saved her own life.

She'd suffered from anxiety for as long as she could remember. An only child, she rarely left the house. She was not allowed to play outside. Everything outdoors was a potential threat. And some things indoors too. Once, when she discovered a housefly buzzing about in a bedroom, she closed up that room for a week, hoping the offending insect would die a natural death.

Whether Penney's persistent apprehension was caused or merely exacerbated by an excessively protective mother would be hard to say. Her life was very safe, although she never *felt* safe. It was also uneventful. When she turned 18, she was still anxious about everything. She realized how easy it would be to stay home forever. That, without some sort of dramatic intervention, she would never go anywhere. Or do anything. Or become anyone.

So she enlisted in the U.S. Army.

"I knew that if I joined the military, they wouldn't let me stay in my room, hiding in my bed all day," Penney said. She'd been constantly afraid to do anything. In a regimented environment, she'd be afraid to *not* do things.

Somewhere, somehow, she married a fellow soldier along the way. A nice guy. He cared deeply about her. But he had trouble coaxing her to break out of her routines. To socialize or travel. Penney was able to function at her job, but she didn't want to go anywhere other than to work and back home, nor would she talk to strangers unless absolutely required. She had panic attacks and obsessed about so many things.

"I love you. I'll never divorce you," her husband said, "but I'm not sure I can live with you like this."

That's how Penney ended up in an anxiety counseling group. In a roomful of women who were all afraid of something. Who had been violated as children. Who had out-of-body sensations when they felt threatened. Whose ears began to hum when instructions got overwhelming. Who got a metallic taste in their mouths when a panic attack was coming on. Who avoided strangers. Or refused medical treatment. Women who suffered anxiety but were taking a step toward saving their own lives.

᙮I᙮

ALL THINGS TO ALL MEN

Spring forward. Fall back. Or was it the other way around? It might not matter if you forgot it was clock-changing weekend. By Monday, you typically had it sorted out. But if you were a churchgoer, you needed to know the correct time by Sunday morning. Otherwise, you might drive to a deserted parking lot or arrive to a throng of worshippers exiting when you're trying to enter.

Protestant church service at the post chapel started at 10 a.m. Disoriented by having arrived a couple of minutes late, I slipped into a back pew and reached for a hymnal. People next to me were kneeling and crossing themselves and murmuring phrases I hadn't heard since childhood when my mother's friend Robin would take me to Mass with her. Was this a Catholic service? I glanced at my watch. Had the schedule changed? No, the clocks had. All except mine.

The following week, I intentionally attended both types of worship. Maybe I could score extra brownie points in heaven like my Uncle Homer who, diagnosed with lung cancer, accepted visits from every type of clergy at the hospital. Jewish, Baptist, Presbyterian. He said he couldn't be sure who was right, so he was acquiring a range of fire insurance policies. When the priest stopped by, Homer asked him to hear his and Aunt Mildred's vows. Forty years after their original wedding, he wanted to be married in the Catholic tradition of his youth.

Between the two types of service at the military chapel, a transformation takes place. As the Protestant chaplain in a simple black robe leads the recessional toward the back of the church, boys in robes appear from the wings at the front of the church like members of a prop crew springing into action between scenes of a play.

Chapel assistants bring in statues of Jesus and the Virgin Mary. Others move chairs from their positions in front of the altar to stations behind the pulpit. They take away the flowers and swap short, thick votive candles at the back of the altar for tall, tapered ones at the front. The Bible and offering trays are removed.

A child makes his way around the perimeter of the chapel. In his white robe, holding a long pole with a hook at one end, he looks rather like some brass-angel tree ornament. His job is to ready fourteen wooden cases along the wall that open to reveal the stations of the cross.

In five minutes, a chapel full of Protestant symbols has become a suitable setting for a Catholic Mass. One final gesture remains. The culminating act is the transformation of the massive wooden cross. It hangs, suspended from a ceiling bracket. Chaplain's assistants reach up and rotate the cross from a plain face bearing the letters INRI to reveal a crucifix where Jesus hangs, bleeding.

In an hour, the process will repeat itself in reverse. A medley of silver trays and trappings will be exchanged. The stations of the cross will be closed. The cross will be rotated to depict not the dying Savior but a resurrected Lord, as Protestants like to say.

The chapel staff will have executed their well designed plan. Throughout the week, choir practices will be held, confessions heard, social hours hosted, and weddings performed. All in the little square structure with a needle-like spire that ends neither in a cross nor in a weathervane but in a simple point.

Following the example of Saint Paul, the army chapel attempts to be all things to all people, changing its colors and its clergy every day of the week and at least twice on Sunday.

◦∤◦

A CHAPLAIN FOR ALL SEASONS

The chaplain serves parishioners of many persuasions in the course of a week. He must develop a philosophy that allows him to live his convictions while helping others live theirs. His role is unique among officers: He or she is a soldier but principally a pastor.

A chaplain I interviewed had entered the army during the Vietnam era, but when I met him he was serving in Heidelberg. His staff worked primarily with the big three: Catholic, Protestant, and Jewish. They coordinated with other faith groups including Muslim, Seventh Day Adventist, and Latter-Day Saint, but those communities got lower priority in use of facilities and tended to meet off-post. His community included 1,200 Protestants from thirty denominations. How do you teach Sunday School to children from every background? A chaplain's board may decide that this year's Lutheran lessons are the best available for third graders but choose Southern Baptist literature for the fifth graders.

Protestant Sunday ritual shifts dramatically throughout the year.

"Our cliché is that, during the main part of the year, we are Presbyterian or Methodist. During the summer, we're

Baptist. During liturgical seasons like Lent, we become Episcopal."

Greater divergence arises at Christmastime. Catholics may fall into a somber Advent season, while exuberant Protestants are eager to haul out their trees, lights, and wreaths. Sanctuary decorating becomes problematic. The chapel staff usually end up decorating one week later than the Protestants would like, which is one week earlier than the Catholics would prefer.

Thanksgiving is surprisingly challenging because it's "a patriotic day with religious significance for most people," the chaplain said, but many observers of the feast are not Christian, so the services are ecumenical. For such gatherings, the chapel's heavy wooden cross is removed from sight.

"There's a part of me that resists that," the Christian pastor soldier admitted, "but it's all a part of the respect we give one another."

"Careful attention to detail is required even though some things may seem trivial," he said. "All worship traditions are a gift of God. If you've got the right people, you can successfully make those decisions with love."

⁓!⁓

LIFE IN GERMANY

HIGH-FUNCTIONING ALCOHOLIC

One winter, our friend Frankie began suffering from thick red sores at the corners of his mouth. Not chapped lips. Not fever blisters. The lesions looked like something I'd once seen in a nutrition textbook: cheilosis. It's caused by a deficiency in vitamin B2. That, in turn, was caused by drinking too much alcohol. The patient eventually improved, not because he stopped drinking but because his doctor prescribed riboflavin supplements.

Frankie was an alcoholic by his own admission, but he functioned well at work. In fact, he was excellent at his job. A retired master sergeant transferred from Rock Island, he put in a full, productive day managing government communications. He could and would do anything needed. Meetings. Memos. Reports. Phone calls. Budgets. No complaints, no whining, no excuses, no temper tantrums. He just got it done. Put in a solid eight hours.

Then he'd go to the Altdeutsche Bierstube and drink beer all evening. He was home in time to say goodnight to his children, sleep off the haze, and be at work, punctual and alert, in the morning. Frankie was such a regular at the Altdeutsche that he was on a first-name basis with many of the local regulars. Even though he was an American, even though he spoke their language poorly and carelessly, slurring over definite articles so they all sounded like *"da,"* he had earned a place at their *stammtisch*. In any *bierstube* was a special table reserved for a particular group of regulars. Large and round, it stood out from the smaller rectangular tables and was reserved for the most-devoted clientele, whether they showed up that night or not. It had a more ornate tablecloth and a unique centerpiece, and anyone not part of the gang knew better than to sit there. They essentially owned that table and furthermore, being German, each had his own position at that table. Helmut sat to the right of Gerhardt, Gerhardt sat to the right of Juergen, Juergen sat to the right of Erik, and so forth. Having a German wife and having lived in-country for decades, Frankie had earned the right to sit to the right of Erik and play cards and discuss politics and tell jokes.

One evening, Frankie arrived early feeling a bit cheeky. He didn't have to tell Carla that he wanted a Pils. Carla. Terse, angular, too-skinny Carla with the too-black hair understood his broken dialect. She knew what he wanted to drink. The *stammtisch* was empty, and he strode directly to the group table and made himself comfortable. With a sly wink at Carla, he slid into Georg's chair closest to the window. When a couple of the regulars came in expecting to assume their customary seats, they were stunned. Frankie was in someone else's place, and now nobody knew where to sit. They stood awkwardly. Frankie gave them an innocent look. The Germans looked at Carla, then at the proprietor. How could they have let this happen? Why had this friend done such a thing? What should they do now? After a few painful moments, Frankie burst out laughing, his beer belly shaking. He stood up and moved to his own seat. *Alles in ordnung.* Symmetry restored.

GERMAN MEN DO KEGEL
EXERCISES

W hen the good times were rolling at the Altdeutsche Bierstube, you could hear the merriment a block away. There was a warm glow in the steamy windows and on the rosy faces in the smoky *wirtschaft*.

Altdeutsche was not your typical *gemütliches gasthaus*. It was kind of raucous. For years, it appealed to local citizenry with their regular table as well as to GIs with beer that was actually served cold, in the American tradition. When you walked through the door, you said *guten abend* to no one in particular, and there was a murmured reply. You could stop by the Altdeutsche after work any day of the week and, for a few deutschmarks, enjoy one of two main-dish selections. The specialty of the day might be fried fish and an excellent potato salad prepared with oil and vinegar, not mayonnaise. Or there could be *gulaschsuppe* or *würstchen mit sauerkraut*. If the day's menu didn't suit your tastes, you could always order *schnitzel:* the omnipresent breaded-and-fried pork cutlet.

Up at the counter, three or four men would be rolling dice in a cup, the loser of each game paying for a round of *Berg-Bräu Leimen Bier*.

At the *stammtisch,* a half dozen regular customers would be playing cards. The group's accordionist might be there providing free entertainment for everyone.

On Monday evenings, a bunch of American contractors met at the pub for *kegeln.* This kind of kegel has nothing to do with pelvic-floor exercises for incontinent women. It's a type of nine-pin bowling. If you wanted to go bowling, you needed to find the lane. To get to it, you had to go through the ladies' room. More precisely, through the door labeled "*Damen,*" then past but not through the bathroom entrance, then outside and down the steps to an alley where a feral mama cat hissed and snatched a straying kitten back into the shadows. And then into the light of the smoke-filled *kegelbahn.*

The game hall at the Altdeutsche consisted of a single lane with a chalkboard for keeping score. The game was played with heavy plastic balls about six inches in diameter. Some had two finger holes; some had none. Nine kegel pins were set up in a square, dangling from strings like puppets so they were easily reset.

There were no teams. Participants played various games with different scoring methods every round. In one game, players started out owing three deutschmarks to the money jar. If you knocked down five pins or none at all, you owed an additional fifty pfennigs. For any other count, you were credited ten pfennigs per pin. The first player to achieve a zero balance would win. This could make for an extended evening.

In a different kegel game, a designated "fox" rolled first, and all the other players aimed to beat his score. If you tied the fox, both of you paid ten pfennigs to the common fund. If you played better than the fox, he had to pay ten pfennigs per pin advantage. If you played worse, you owed the ten-cent fines.

At evening's end, all scores and debts are settled. It doesn't much matter whether you break even or not. Whatever you lose goes into the "kitty" to pay for a dinner party at the end of the season. In that sense, everybody wins.

‹۱›

GUEST WORKER

Exotic strains of music drifted through the open doorway to the back room of the restaurant. Spicy meats were grilling. Perky fresh flowers graced the tables. Wine glasses were clinking.

"Prost!" the German language teacher exclaimed. *"Prost,"* I returned the toast, lifting a cognac snifter to my lips. The *weinbrand* burned its way down my uninitiated throat, flushing my cheeks and softening my vision of the floral wallpaper and pewter wall hangings in the Mainzer Rad restaurant.

Christian, the restaurateur, was friendly and enjoyed regular patronage by Americans. This evening he provided complimentary servings of the after-dinner drink as his contribution to our little graduation celebration. A dozen of us had completed a government-sponsored Gateway to German course.

The teacher was Sylvia, a Hispanic woman from New Mexico who had married a local national. When Christian returned to the kitchen, Sylvia told us that there was a movement underfoot to oust residents like him. He was a *gastarbeiter*, a guest worker. In the 1960s, Germany had welcomed workers from Yugoslavia and other countries, men and women willing to work for low wages at jobs that

German citizens did not particularly want. By the 1980s, conditions had reversed; the country was suffering from high unemployment. Some people felt that whatever jobs were available should go to local workers.

"There has even been talk in government circles of paying these people to go back home," Teacher continued, "but of course they don't want to go. This is their home. Look at Christian: He speaks almost-perfect *Deutsch;* his children go to school here. How could he possibly go back to Yugoslavia now?"

AN AMERICAN IN AMERICA

Alonzo was born a citizen of the USA, but he didn't set foot there until he was 22. When he finally got to America, his experiences left him alternately impressed, enlightened, embarrassed, and bemused.

Alonzo's mother was from Spain, and that's where he was born. His father had been an American sailor stationed in Rota. That status gave his son the right to U.S. citizenship. When the family moved to Germany, Alonzo attended local schools, grew up multilingual, and got a job with a U.S. contractor. He considered himself European but figured he ought to see his supposed homeland. His best friend, Kai, was employed by the German government, so the young men saved up some money and vacation days and decided to see the USA in a rented Chevrolet.

Their loosely set itinerary included such famous tourist attractions as the Empire State Building and Disney World. They seemed even more excited to experience something they'd heard about but could scarcely believe: grocery stores that were open all night. "There we were, buying bread and produce at 10 p.m. That wiped us out! And shopping malls. I never saw anything like it! They're so comfortable and handy." Alonzo had Kai take his picture in the dark in the parking lot of a 7-Eleven convenience-store.

He was like a child who sets aside a new toy to play with the box it came in.

"I understand Japanese tourists now," Alonzo said. "They come to Europe and take pictures of all these boring, everyday things. But we were doing that in America."

At a family-owned restaurant, the two travelers photographed one another eating a real American breakfast: bacon and eggs with a stack of pancakes. The waitress kept bringing them water and refills on coffee. They grew anxious that the beverages were going to end up costing more than the meal. Finally, they asked her to please stop, and she said, "It's free, you know." They didn't know. In several instances, Alonzo's communication was actually hindered by his accent-free English. Americans were used to naïveté and strange questions from tourists but not from an apparent native.

At a doughnut shop, they were beyond impressed when three uniformed policemen sidled up to the long Formica counter for a morning coffee break. "Just like on TV," they whispered to each other.

Luckily, they hadn't encountered any law enforcement when Alonzo approached his first American traffic intersection and pulled his Chevy all the way forward to line up with the signal light. In a German village, this would stop you before the crosswalk; in the U.S., it landed him in the middle of an intersection.

The travelers headed south. Hoping for a scenic drive, they'd gone out of their way to include routes labeled on the map as "toll" roads. These highways turned out to be disappointingly unpleasant – and expensive too. In German, the word *toll* means great, fantastic, stunning.

When the guys got to Alonzo's aunt's house in Alabama, they discovered some unexpected aspects of U.S. housing: push-lock doorknobs, toilet bowls filled with water, and garbage disposals.

"We were feeding food down something called an InSinkErator just to watch it work. Then we started wondering, where does it go?"

They made it to Florida and the Epcot Center and, three weeks after arriving in New York City, Alonzo and Kai left the cyan skies of Miami, crossed back over the Atlantic, and descended through gray clouds into Frankfurt. To get back to his home, Germany, Alonzo was obliged to show his passport. His U.S. passport.

Visiting America was a great experience, he said. "Actually living there would take some adjustment."

⌒I⌒

SUNDAY REGIMEN

Volker got married when he was thirty years old and didn't become a father until he was forty. His wife was an affable British woman with a delightful sense of humor. They met when he was in the U.S. Army in Germany and she was a teenaged nanny to a wealthy family in Stuttgart. He was bilingual, having grown up in the USA with German parents. They were unaffectionate, he complained, and only kept him around so they had someone to pop downstairs and fetch *keller-kalt bier*. Beer at the ideal temperature. Volker was an only child, and he didn't want a similar environment for his daughter, Rebecca. He and his wife hoped to eventually produce a sibling for her. Volker adored his daughter, enjoyed seeing her dance in front of the sliding glass door, watching her own mirrored image. Aiming to be more engaged with his family than his parents had been, he had told the obstetrician he wanted to be present for his wife's labor and delivery. The request was flatly denied. "You are way too large," the hospital staff informed him. "If you faint, no one here can lift you out of the way."

Volker had no prior experience parenting or even babysitting. One Saturday morning, when Diane was out, he played with his toddler, cleaned up the house, and did some light yard work. After an hour or two, he sank breathlessly into a chair with a fresh cup of coffee. He was pretty satisfied with himself. His wife should be pleased with him when she got back. He relaxed into the soft chair and closed his eyes for a moment.

"*Wasser, bitte?*" A tiny plaintiff voice was coming from somewhere in the vicinity of his left knee. He opened his eyes, startled, and realized that Rebecca's mother had been gone for four hours, and he'd not given the child so much as a biscuit or a cup of juice. He'd made himself a cup of coffee and not offered her a glass of water. She didn't cry or complain; it was just a question. May I have some water? Which of course made him feel extra guilty.

Maybe he'd take her upstairs before Mum came home and change her into one of those lacy little dresses. They were cute enough frocks, he supposed, though he couldn't understand why most of them were gray. What kind of hue was that for a child to wear?

In fact, the baby clothes were mostly pink. Volker was colorblind. It hadn't taken long for his colleagues to figure this out.

"Hey, Volker, was your wife mad at you this morning?"

"I don't think so. Why?"

"Because you're wearing a turquoise shirt with powder-blue pants. And a green necktie."

Everyone loved Diane and thought Volker was lucky she put up with him. Although he grumbled a lot, Volker often displayed an enviable, almost childlike enjoyment of life.

One thing he delighted in was food and, like a lot of retired soldiers, he packed on quite a few pounds as soon as he stopped having to do official weigh-ins. Diane learned his secret to losing his fighting-weight physique while they were living in the United States. She too had what the French might call *un bon coup de fourchette*, and they got into the habit of indulging in freshly made doughnuts on weekends. Volker would go pick up the Krispy Kremes, apparently eating a couple of them right out of the box while driving home.

One weekend, when he was gone, Diane decided she'd stop by and get the glazed pastries. She ordered a box of a dozen and mentioned that her husband, Volker, was usually the one who picked them up.

"Only *one* dozen today then?" the shop owner asked. "Your husband always buys two."

PUSHING BUTTONS

"Oooh, your chicken's red!" Rosie, five, felt it was her duty as the older, wiser sibling to point this out to three-year-old Brett. We were at an Indian restaurant on East Sixth Street in Manhattan, and the children's mother thought everyone would savor the curry except her little boy. The waitress suggested a bowl of plain chicken with white rice.

This was the summer I spent living in Greenwich Village and working at Young & Rubicam. I was honored that my former professor, a Madison Avenue alumna, and her husband would meet me "in the city," as they say. One night we saw *The Sisters Rosensweig* on Broadway. On this occasion, though, they had brought their children so we could all dine together. All was well as the meal began. Brett's tandoori chicken tasted mild, and he was happy with it until his older sister remarked on its bright red color. He stopped eating and put down his fork.

"Yeah. You're right." That was it. He wouldn't eat another bite.

Siblings have an innate knack for pushing each other's buttons. It must be a universal instinct that children are born with, for a similar thing happened with friends of ours overseas. Grace loved shopping. For Hummel figurines.

Swarovski crystal. Turkish rugs. Käthe Wohlfahrt ornaments. She hadn't been able to go to the famous Christkindlesmarkt in Nuremberg their first winters overseas because they had an infant son. Now, Johann, so named for having been born in Germany, was two years old, and the parents made a deal: They'd get a hotel and Dad would entertain Johann and his older sister, Amy, while Mom spent bustling days shopping at the outdoor stalls filled with Black Forest raspberry candies, gingerbread, and *spekulatius* almond cookies. She'd buy family gifts of sherpa-lined mittens, wooden clocks, handmade toys, and knitted caps. Her idea of a cruel joke was to buy her sister-in-law a Hummel ashtray on the grounds that it was too cute to use and would induce the woman to quit smoking. At the end of the day, she'd sip a mug of hot mulled *glühwein* and bring back dried sausages for Henry.

Grace got up early, dressed quickly, and slipped quietly out of the hotel. She would shop all morning and afternoon, then come meet Henry and the kids for an early dinner out. The hope was that Amy and Johann would sleep late, and then Dad would offer them various diversions throughout the day. Johann woke up and was immediately handed his blue Care Bear. Before he could tire of that, Dad brought out his Tonka trucks and tractors. He was contentedly rolling a bright-yellow dump truck up and down the hills and valleys in the puffy down quilt when Amy woke up. Six years old, she'd been briefed on the situation the night before. Dad held his finger to his pursed lips and gave her the "shhh" reminder.

Amy immediately rolled over in bed, poked her brother on his arm, and announced, "Bad news, Johann: Mama's gone!"

Dad winced. The little guy set down his toys and glanced around the room. He ran into the bathroom, and he looked in the *schrank*. Then his chin began to tremble, and his big eyes filled with tears.

No one knows how to get to a fella quite like an older sister.

᭡

I COULDN'T NOT BUY IT

International connections have enriched my life. My experiences with living and traveling abroad have informed my decisions regarding work, both paid and volunteer, my friendships, and my faith. Even my behavior in the marketplace.

One of the first things you have to do when you move to a new city is to choose grocery stores to replace the ones you've grown used to. Shops that carry your preferred selection of culinary staples. Returning to the States, it took us a couple of months to find a nice, big Asian market in Tucson. We picked up packages of ready-made *dal makhani* and *palak paneer*. Mango and lime chutneys. Samosa snacks. When John was already at the cashier counter, he remembered that he'd wanted to check if the shop carried Lee Kum Kee chili sauce. The cashier directed me to a far aisle marked Chinese food. It didn't seem to be there, but it wasn't urgent, so I decided to give up.

Halfway down the row of colorfully laden shelves, I heard a man call out something, but I assumed he was addressing another shopper. By the time I got to the far end of the aisle, I realized he was talking to me. It was the bagboy, and he wanted to tell me the Lee Kum Kee was actually on the opposite side of the store. John had already finished checking out by then, but I headed off in the direction indicated so the guy would think I was going to pick it up even though I had decided not to. No such luck. The clerk decided to take me there. He led me along the back of the store, past the refrigerated units, the Indian aisle, the Indonesian aisle, the Thai food, Taiwanese food, Cambodian and Caribbean groceries, over to the very last aisle, and back up toward the front of the store. There sat the product, in its slim orange bottle, on a lower shelf. OK, good to know; I'll get it next time. But the boy was still watching me, so I picked up a bottle and carried it to the cash register to pay for it.

What compelled to make that purchase? Amarula...

A popular store in the Mannheim area was the Wertkauf hypermarket. It was Walmart, Home Depot, Costco, and Ikea all in one. A furniture store and some smaller shops were attached by covered walkways, and John liked to stop for a currywurst at a kiosk in the shade. This glorified hotdog was served on a crisp *brötchen* in place of a wimpy Holsum bun, and it was drizzled with dark-red sauce and sprinkled with bright-copper curry powder. Inside Wertkauf there were samples of foods and beverages on special promotion.

We had a shopping list and a big cart filled with stuff. A long cardboard box with a build-it-yourself *schrank* for the bathroom. A crusty loaf of wholegrain bread. Bottles of spiced apple rings. Greek feta and olives packed in oil and herbs. Fruits and salad vegetables. Packages of fresh pork.

On our way to look for artichokes, we were offered taste samples including a little glass of Amarula. New to me then, this liqueur is similar to Irish cream, but it's made with fruit of the South African marula or elephant tree. The shapely bottle was made of brown glass and labeled with a gold-framed picture of the marula fruit and a large-eared elephant. A bright-yellow rope with tassels was tied jauntily around the neck of the bottle. There was supposed to be a little plastic elephant magnet on it too, but the representative handing out the samples said she had just run out of them.

John enjoyed the sample (free alcohol at a family grocery store) and set a bottle in our shopping basket. I gave him the look: *Yes, it's yummy, but we don't need it. How many deutschmarks does that cost anyway?* After we'd rounded a corner, out of sight of the saleswoman, I ditched the bottle on a random shelf and continued toward the row of checkout stands. He went back and retrieved the bottle. *Fine, I give in.* Good thing too, because, while we were waiting in line, the Amarula woman came racing over to us. She'd found an extra elephant and been rushing through the store looking for us so she could tie the plastic magnet around the bottle with a bright-yellow rope.

Whew! Diplomatic crisis averted.

And that's why, years later, I had to buy the Lee Kum Kee sauce in Tucson, Arizona.

~❡~

PROGRAMMING IN THE PUBLIC INTEREST

The housing agent said he didn't know whether we would be able to get the Armed Forces Network signal in our apartment.

"My wife and I don't care about TV," he sniffed.

Vegetating in front of the television may seem especially shameful if you're living in the cultural cornucopia of Europe. We should be making the most of every sightseeing minute, every historically significant second.

The truth was, we couldn't spend every moment broadening our horizons. Daily life and routine office jobs could resemble the old description of war: hours of boredom punctuated by, in our case, sheer excitement.

You can't be visiting Nuremberg, touring Neuschwanstein, or eating tiramisu all the time. We watched what programming was available. Here's what AFN aired:

ABC Nightline came on at 7 a.m. with news and insight from Ted Koppel. The NBC Today show wished us a good morning as we were coming home from work. Popular afternoon talk shows aired four weeks later than in the States. Weekly news-magazine shows like *60 Minutes* ran one week late. *The Tonight Show* was not on regularly, so you couldn't count on falling asleep with Johnny Carson.

Sudsy dramas broadcast by the American station in Europe included *General Hospital* in the afternoon and *Dallas* in the evening, both several months delayed. Soap opera plots unfold pretty slowly anyway, so it may have been hard to notice. A Screen Actors Guild strike postponed for months the revelation of who shot *Dallas*'s J.R. Ewing in Texas, but the wait was longer in Rhineland Pfalz. That cliff-hanger was the subject of Monday morning watercooler talk, along with anticipation of Monday night football to be aired eighteen hours late. Followers of those programs would warn their stateside families: Do not reveal the outcome! One sports event, the Game of the Week, was broadcast live, but you had to stay up until 2 a.m. to catch it – even if you were a soldier who had to be at work, and presumably alert, at 7:30 a.m.

Some popular shows were picked up by AFN several seasons into their inception, so you didn't get to see the pilot episode. When you transferred back to the USA, you'd miss intervening seasons and would never catch up.

Shows we got were either extremely popular must-haves in the USA or shows so exceedingly poor they'd been cancelled after a single season and were easily dumped on the nonprofit market.

Most programming ran at odd hours. Because AFN carried no advertising, *Murder She Wrote* might start at 7:50 and run until 8:30. It made you aware of how much – or how little – actual entertainment was in an hourlong show. Just when you got used to *MacGyver's* being on Tuesday evening, it stopped altogether, replaced by some fake-fur alien, and reappeared months later but on Wednesdays.

The TV spots we came to call "AFN commercials" were not commercials at all, because the Armed Forces Network was funded by taxes rather than advertisements. Between-show messages were not attempts to persuade us in favor of one brand of soap over another. We were, instead, exhorted to guard national secrets and be good international guests.

The message strategy could be worthwhile.

Why use two when one will do? A reminder about paper towel waste in the lavatories.

He's not going to like this. But he's going to have to see it. Advice on telling your superior officers the truth even when it hurts.

Don't attend foreign political demonstrations in your military uniform. That one should go without saying.

Most of the message executions were vapid.

A guy in a crew cut stands outside the Morale, Welfare, and Recreation Center asking passersby to accompany him inside. *It's OK. You can come in all by yourself.*

Don't use the staircase as a storage place; you could trip on things.

Don't waste gallons of water from the garden hose to chase away a single tree leaf. How many takes did they film of that guy dramatizing the problem?

A male airman tries to chat up a female airman at a gas station. He's complimenting her wheels and complaining about gasoline prices and having to fill his hot rod's gas tank every week. She tells him that avoiding jackrabbit starts and stops might help. At the end of the message, he hopes he'll see her there again next week. "I only refuel every *two* weeks," she informs him crisply. As though a person made appointments to fill a gas tank.

Since the messages were staged and sponsored by the U.S. government, there was little enthusiasm for spots that featured smiling construction workers thanking soldiers and airmen for defending democracy overseas and singing, "We're behind you."

"Yeah, way behind us," one G.I. complained. "About 4,000 miles away from the Fulda Gap," where it was widely believed during the Cold War that Soviet forces might launch an invasion into Western Europe. "They're paying these actors with tax dollars skimmed off the tops of our paychecks to encourage us to stay here."

Well, they weren't paying for especially talented actors. Or writers.

Another message some soldiers received with skepticism lauded the American presence for its contribution to "the longest peace in Europe in this century." It touted forty years of peace.

On cold winter nights, when the sun set early, we could read or watch television. We watched German TV to improve our listening and speaking skills. When we lived where AFN was available, we watched that too. Still, the longer we were overseas, the larger the gaps grew in our awareness of popular culture back home.

We'd been to the Louvre, but we had no idea who and what was nominated for an Oscar.

We'd shopped at Berlin's 645,834-square-foot *KaDeWe*, but we didn't know what a Cabbage Patch doll was nor why shoppers were fighting over them. (After I eventually saw one, I still couldn't figure it out what the fuss was all about.)

We were able to see the Super Bowl in real time but not the most interesting part: great commercials.

◦⌇◦

THE $64,000 QUESTION

Ethyn was puzzled by German television. He recognized Sesame Street characters, but he couldn't understand them. "What say, Mama?" the toddler would repeatedly ask.

Our first year abroad, we weren't doing significantly better than Ethyn. Even though we understood little of what went on, we watched local television stations. It was all that was available to us initially, and it was a relatively painless way to practice a language.

Local news programs, though important, were exceedingly difficult to understand. The announcers spoke fast, they used sophisticated vocabulary, and visual cues were minimal. Fiction was easier, especially if it was American to start with. Quite a number of detective and adventure series were dubbed into German. Old *Kojak* episodes ran late on Wednesdays. Though the baldheaded detective appeared to speak German, he never did trade in his lollipops for Gummy Bears.

Not as many comedies made it across the Atlantic Ocean. When there were American sitcoms, though, they were the easiest to understand. Something like *The Cosby Show,* once highly popular in a dozen languages and countries, was easy to follow because of its simple phrases, relatively direct translations, and familiar context.

134

Lots of older Hollywood films found their way onto European television. John Wayne movies aired frequently. Some viewers admired the range of his acting ability because he appeared in westerns, war pictures, and other genres. Other critics said he played John Wayne no matter what film he was in. In any case, he proved to be about as versatile an actor in German as he was in English.

Unfamiliar movies led us to make a game of identifying country of origin.

Films featuring famous American actors were too easy. You got no points for recognizing those. Musicals were dead giveaways, as the dialogue might be dubbed with well matched voices, but the original vocal soundtracks for the songs were used.

Sometimes there were other easy clues, such as national monuments in Italy, road signs in French, or cars driving on the left side of the road. A European license plate was evident by its long, horizontal format, but you still had to figure out the country it came from. Makes of cars provided hints, as did yellow headlights, which were exclusive to French vehicles.

Clothing might help. A male actor wearing a letter sweater was probably in the USA.

If a dinner scene failed to feature several bottles of wine on the table, the film was probably American. Breads could be a helpful indicator: the long baguette was French; the sliced, white stuff was American. A dining room with patterned wallpaper would be European. A grandfather clock could throw you off. It might well be German, but it could be gracing a home in America. If we could catch a glimpse of electrical outlets on the walls, we could quickly tell if they were European. Germans, by the way, make the best plugs and outlets in the world: safe, sturdy, and compact.

If we'd exhausted all other clues, we would listen carefully to actors' references to one another. A character named Otto or Gaston would reveal nationality pretty quickly.

Of course, there was the possibility that a film that aired in Germany had actually been domestically produced. To rule out this possibility, we immediately checked for lip sync. The demands of meaning and inflection were usually met, but mouths could not consistently move the right way at the right time in another language. In the worst cases, the speech might continue after the actor's mouth had closed, or his lips would keep forming silent syllables after his voice had stopped.

Game shows were emulated, not translated, so there was no guessing about origin. They were fun in their own right, even if you couldn't understand them. Some were punctuated with numbers performed by a rock band or by other musical entertainment. Definitely not an American format.

This was no place to be a couch potato. Television watching was too much like work.

∽⫯∾

IN OTHER VIEWS

....

PASSION PLAY

*"The only thing necessary for the triumph of
evil is for good men to do nothing."*
(Often attributed to Edmund Burke)

There is something curiously thematic about visiting
a concentration camp and attending a Passion Play
in the same weekend, and a bus tour to Bavaria may
allow you to do that.

In the stage depiction of Christian Holy Week, Pontius
Pilate literally washed his hands in the trial of a first-
century Jew named Jesus and stood by while His enemies
executed Him. Two thousand years later, entire countries
figuratively washed their hands and stood by while millions
of twentieth-century Jews were executed in the Holocaust.

Four hundred years ago, people in Bavaria sought to
make a bargain with God. They established what would
become one of the world's best-known Passion Plays. In the
seventeenth century, it was not uncommon for
communities to make vows in gratitude for – or in a bid
for – God's mercy. The Oberammergau event premiered in
1634 as a pledge against the Black Plague that swept across
Europe in the fourteenth through eighteenth centuries.
From a population of 1,560, more than 300 had been lost to

the dreaded disease. Survivors vowed to enact the religious history every decade in exchange for immunity. Residents felt their deal had been honored. Spared further loss, they continued the decennial performances although not as faithfully as conventional tellings might have us believe. Sixty-seven people involved in the Oberammergau play did not return from World War I. An official play guide asserts that "a play in 1920 was not to be thought of." It also notes: "The play had to be omitted in 1940."

A vow is a vow, is it not? One might think that war and Holocaust would be reasons as profound and compelling as a plague for making a special appeal to God. It would seem that if only seven persons in Oberammergau survived to the end of a decade, then seven persons should stage a Passion Play.

Performers must be ten-year residents of the municipality. An inhabitant might be among a crowd of children on the stage at a performance, claim the role of a disciple a decade later, and eventually portray a senior member of the Sanhedrin. The year I attended saw controversy in the casting of Mary, mother of Jesus. The person assigned the role was a married woman. Probably not a virgin.

Motionless depictions in the Living Tableaux represented Old Testament scenes. These foreshadowed New Testament fulfillment of prophecies acted out over a six-hour period. The vocalists were impressive, the orchestra faultless. Precision was noticeably lacking from chorus line movements, however, and the acting was lackluster.

The event is not a profit-making venture, although local shops do a booming business in religious and tourist items including the wood carvings for which the region is famous. In fact, the director of the play when I was there was a Bavarian wood carver, Han Maier.

Accommodating changing perspectives, the Oberammergau script has been rewritten numerous times. The version I saw was based on Father Othmar Weis' ideas for "the removal of so-called antisemitic passages as well as adjustments made in conformity with the wishes of the Second Vatican Council," according to an English-language guide. "All of those passages which might give even the slightest appearance of offence to the Jewish people have now been expurgated from the new Play-book. In many places, the new text depends more clearly on the Bible words so as to forestall any prejudgments."

The Passion Play is now based on the Bible? What an inspired idea.

᭡

ELKE FROM THE EAST

"**G**et out of East Germany now. Escape while you can," the young man warned Elke. She was not safe. He had reason to know. He was the one who had betrayed her.

Elke was born in Berlin when World War II was raging. By the time she was in her teens, a 96-mile-long wall had been erected around and through the capital city, and her family found themselves living in communist Germany. Circumstances were difficult, propaganda reached ridiculous levels, and people were fearful, she recalled. They were hungry too, and everyone had to help. One of her early jobs was on a farm.

"There were these potato bugs we had to pick every day to preserve the crop, and we were told they had been dropped by the U.S. Air Force," she said. "Even as a child, I didn't believe that."

In spite of Cold War conditions, Elke continued her education. As she neared completion, her future became less certain. You are not politically fit for graduation, the school administration threatened. She and her parents worried for weeks about her fate, wondering what had prompted such a damning evaluation.

As it turned out, a neighbor had reported her to the authorities. Peter had emigrated several times back and forth across the line between East and West Germany, and the authorities were either suspicious of his motives or tired of his being a nuisance. Once he finally made up his mind to stay in the East, he sought to improve his flagging image. A well known means of ingratiating oneself and demonstrating loyalty was to report someone else for disloyal activities. Peter informed local political party officials that he had seen Elke get off a bus in West Berlin, repeatedly making contact with the same stranger. Now she was being investigated. That was the source of her problem, but she didn't know how to defend herself – or even that she needed to do so.

When it was determined that she would likely graduate after all, her parents hosted a celebration in their home. One of Elke's closest girlfriends brought an escort to the event: Peter. It was a lovely party where warm friendship and well wishes combined with relief until late in the evening. Before it was over, Elke noticed Peter sitting alone on the front porch, looking befuddled.

"I can't believe it." He shook his head. "You're so nice, you and your family," he told Elke. "I must give you some advice: Get to the West side. Soon."

She fled within two weeks.

⌐I⌐

QUASI-ADVENTURE THROUGH
EAST GERMANY

"**D**on't go see the wall," Gretchen advised us before our trip to Berlin. "It's sad and will cloud the rest of your stay here." She saw it when she was sixteen. Intended as an entertaining adventure with some teenaged friends from West Germany, it turned out to be educational and sobering.

"We were allowed to cross into the East and go to a restaurant there," Gretchen recounted, "but West German youths were not permitted to mingle with East German youths. Not even for a quick, casual hello. They had to sit at separate tables. I think it's very sad."

She rarely went back. West Germans were offended by several factors, one of those being enforced currency exchanges. Money from the East was worth a tenth of that on the West side, so U.S. tourists could indulge in a sumptuous meal for a couple of dollars on the other side of the wall. West German citizens, however, were obliged to change a certain minimum of currency at the border – at a grossly overrated one-to-one exchange rate. The policy was a fundraiser for the communist-controlled territory.

They were pleased to bring gifts to their East German family but were disturbed when acquaintances made specific demands. Not just blue jeans, they insisted; Levi's. Not just a new shirt but one emblazoned with the Izod alligator. Bring us good stuff, but park around the block where our neighbors won't see you.

Americans serving in the armed forces were encouraged to visit Berlin because it should intensify their sense of purpose articulated as "defending our way of life." The idea of crossing into this territory was exhilarating, like watching a suspense thriller. You could enjoy being a teeny bit scared when you knew full well that you were perfectly safe.

The duty train departed Frankfurt in the evening. Our fellow passengers were soldiers reporting for duty in U.S.-occupied Berlin. They wore camouflage fatigues and carried their rifles with them. We all showed our official passports. We were lucky to get first-class accommodations due to John's TDY status.

Military and civilians alike submitted to in-briefings at the train station. We were reminded that, to reach the enclave city of West Berlin, we would be crossing throughout the night. No stops would be made en route. No one would be permitted to leave the train. No photos could be taken. The trips were scheduled in darkness because we weren't supposed to see anything, notice anything, peer out the windows. So, of course that's the first thing I wanted to do. We reclined in our berths, lying under olive-drab wool blankets. Every hour or so, I'd lift the window shade a few centimeters and peer into the darkness. The speed of passage helped obscure details of what seemed to be small white buildings, metal sheds, and fences. No announcement was made, so we never knew when we crossed from West Germany into East. By the time it was light enough to see, we were in West Berlin.

Bolstered by coffee strong enough to compensate for lack of sleep, we set out to see the divided city. John's priority was, as always, to get an overview by walking the length and breadth of the downtown area "to take the measure of the city." We couldn't walk the entire city because it was twenty-one by twenty-seven miles of parks, ponds, and the world's largest zoo. We strolled the two-mile-long Kurfürstendamm, colloquially called Ku'damm. It has also been called the Champs-Élysées of Germany (an exaggerated comparison). We saw Benjamin Franklin Hall, Charlottenburg Palace, and the seamy Potsdamer red-light district. We gazed at the occupying powers' flags: British, French, Soviet and American. Obligatory stops included KaDeWe, the continent's largest department store, and the water-clock tower in Europa-Center.

At the Center, we had to try Berliner Weisse once. Only once. The pink beverage looked lovely and refreshing in plump, inviting goblets, white froth on top. It disappointed us both. John didn't appreciate the raspberry syrup tampering with the taste of real beer. I disliked it because it did still taste like beer.

Americans usually wanted to see the third east/west crossing point. It was named according to the NATO phonetic alphabet: C as in Charlie. A bus from the Ku'damm headed to Friedrichstraße which dead-ended abruptly, interrupted by a concrete edifice. The wall truncated the street like it dissected families.

John was not permitted to cross into the East with an official passport but I, feeling deliciously naughty, hid my red one, and pulled out my blue tourist passport. This allowed me to take an afternoon tour of East Berlin where I saw Stalinist-era office buildings, plain and functional, with tinted glass and some broken windows. Then I passed through the monumental cobalt-blue-tiled Babylonian Ishtar Gate reconstructed inside hallways of the Pergamon Museum. This was an unforgettable experience of walking through time. The East German guide made sure the bus stopped at a café to entice us to spend West German marks before leaving. There wasn't much else we could spend money on: no shops with souvenirs, no picture books, no postcards, no T-shirts.

The Berlin wall was a thirteen-foot-high stucco snake bordered by a no-man's-land once riddled with explosive traps. Television viewers who saw the graffiti on the west side of the barrier couldn't see the east side, which was plain. Barbed wire prevented easterners from approaching to write any sort of protest on it. The Soviet side of the wall, like its news, was whitewashed.

The tour director made sure we saw the damaged tower of Kaiser Wilhelm Memorial Church. Its steeple remains unrepaired "as a reminder against further destruction," our guide said. He made sure we didn't leave the city without stopping to contemplate a wooden cross erected in memory of a family killed trying to escape East Germany in 1980. It is estimated that 600 people died seeking freedom between 1961 and 1989.

THE WALLS COME TUMBLING DOWN

November 9th has often been associated with notable events in German history. Between 1848 and 1989, this date saw leaders displaced, dethroned, and executed. It saw the infamous Kristallnacht. It also saw the fall of the Berlin Wall.

When American educator Roberta heard that the east-west crossing point on Bösebrücke had opened, she hopped on her bicycle to go see for herself. Thousands of families were flooding through the gates, entering a space closed off to them for twenty-eight years. Roberta was witnessing history in the making. The infamous Berlin Wall was suddenly bursting open. It was early evening November 9, 1989.

Traffic was bumper-to-bumper with tiny two-stroke Trabis on *Straße des 17. Juni*, a street named for the day in 1953 when Soviet troops crushed a workers' revolt in East Germany. On this night, it was a street of liberation. Kurfürstendamm boulevard was blocked off to serve as a pedestrian zone. People were laughing and crying and singing.

"I saw some guy sitting on the Ku'damm playing his cello," Roberta said. The next day's newspaper identified him as world-famous Russian cellist Mstislav Rostropovich.

Roberta had called me to describe the scene. "It's very emotional. You glance around, and everyone's eyes are teary. Normally, I find German crowds too aggressive. But people are so happy, so high on freedom right now that everyone is being extra polite."

Later on, there might be misunderstandings over work ethics and schedules. There might be resentment over three decades of inequities. Disagreements about rights and governance and prejudices. But tonight the air was filled with unfettered joy and wonder.

Men from both sides of the wall began dismantling miles of barriers, felling large sections with sledge-hammers. Police monitored from elevated platforms. Not wielding weapons, just watching. The wall had claimed hundreds of lives, and now, destroying it seemed constructive. Walls were coming down. Literally.

Begrüßungsgeld of 100 deutschmarks had traditionally been made available to any East German who could safely make it to the West. Roberta's pathos was aroused as she watched people line up to receive that welcome money, then spend it on coffee, chocolate, and fruit. Who hasn't heard of German chocolate? It's everywhere. Yet for half of the country it had been a rare luxury.

Some newcomers bought electronics. Here and there Roberta would see two men carrying home a television set between them. No looting. No drunken brawls. Many residents crossed to the west side to have a look about. Then they went back home, content in the knowledge that they could come again the next day. All day Friday and Saturday visitors streamed across the breached border. On Sunday the shops opened, a practice generally unheard of.

Even post offices and banks agreed to open on Sunday. The government distributed a record amount of *begrüßungsgeld:* 43.5 million deutschmarks in one weekend. Flyers circulated announcing that East Germans could go to the post office and dial up anyone they wished, at no charge. Free city transportation was offered, and the U-bahns were frightfully crammed with passengers. "I was afraid I'd be inadvertently pushed out at a random stop when the automatic doors opened," Roberta said.

When the weekend was over, the streets were unusually littered with trash, and empty champagne bottles were strewn about. The gates remained open. People continued to pass back and forth. The wall continued to be dismantled.

⁓❢⁓

FALLING IN LOVE

....

WHAT DO THEY WANT FROM US?

Ingrid and Reinhardt invited us to dinner when we first met them at a social meeting of German and American adult students engaged in learning one another's language. The students were all supposed to introduce themselves and their hometowns. My presentation was a show-and-tell featuring handmade Navajo dolls.

Not all Europeans welcome strangers into their homes, so this invitation made an impression. I wore my nicest dress, and John gave flowers to the hostess, as my mother had taught us to do. Language was a barrier, but we managed an engaging conversation with the whole family that lasted until I was falling asleep on my plate. Before the end of the night, our acquaintances proposed meeting at the Backfischfest on the Rhine River. Another day, they took us to what we came to call Hofheim Beach, where twenty or thirty families had wooden huts situated around a manmade lake. There were grills for cooking, boats for paddling, and brilliant geraniums on every deck and dock.

Why are they being so nice to us? We aim to be gracious, but we're not an endlessly fascinating couple.

Military briefings regarding security and espionage had made me slightly suspicious of friendly overtures by "local nationals." Do foreigners ask for details about your job? Do they harbor radical political perspectives? Are they seeking favors?

Soon we were going on volksmarches with them and meeting their jogging club, where participants were grouped by speed and agility. Like most German activities, there was a correct way to do this: rules to be followed, the right clothing, shoes, and gear. The forest paths crisscrossed in a couple of places, and the groups knew exactly when and where to expect to encounter the others. They took great delight in hailing each other at the intersections.

Our new friends thought we might like to try *Ostereierschießen*. Be sure to pronounce this correctly: It's *schieß*, not to be confused with *scheiß*, they hastily corrected us. We surprised them by being pretty decent at shooting the targets and winning colored Easter eggs. *Hey, we're from the gun-happy U.S. of A., are we not?*

I bought peanut butter and Hershey's chocolate for them because Reinhardt remembered getting these things from American soldiers in World War II. It's not that Hershey's was superior to German or Swiss chocolate (*au contraire!*), but it evoked positive memories of an otherwise grim time in his life. (Yes, I actually bought commissary products and gave them to local nationals.)

We were welcome guests at an anniversary party where Ingrid's uncle raided her closet to stage an impromptu fashion show: the other guests modeled while he provided hyperbolic commentary. They took us to their in-laws' Mosel River home one weekend, and we gave the children Lincoln Logs.

I bought tiny Langenscheidt Lilliput dictionaries, keeping the English-German one and giving Ingrid the *Deutsch-Englisch* version. We sat in the back seat of their Volkswagen consulting two-by-two-inch lexicons to facilitate conversation. The road ran parallel to a train track, and Reinhardt promised us a view of the Zugspitze, which was surprising since we weren't going far south enough to see the country's highest mountain. His wife laughed. When we rounded the next curve, there came a locomotive pulling scores of wagons after it. *Die Spitze des Zuges:* the head of a train.

When we passed two cars mangled in a recent autobahn wreck, Ingrid described it as *komisch,* then made sure I knew that the word could mean strange as well as funny. That *is* funny, I said; we have the same concept.

We invited Ingrid and Reinhardt and their daughter for American Thanksgiving, serving potatoes and gravy and turkey (the only time I cooked a turkey in my life). They in turn asked us to Christmas dinner. Serving potatoes and sauce and turkey.

They wished us *Guten Rutsch,* a "good slide" into the new year, inviting us to spend the night. That way we could watch neighbors launching fireworks from high-rise apartment balconies and not have to drive on the autobahn after the Saint Sylvester celebration. Their friends told

Helmut Kohl jokes and asked what we thought of their President and ours.

Before the evening was over, we were introduced to a decades-old tradition: watching *Dinner for One*, a black-and-white English film from the 1960s that had become compulsory holiday fare for millions of Germans.

Ingrid gave us cherries from their tree and a whole set of Mainzelmännchen. The figurines were wrapped in individual wads of gift paper. *Bonbons?* I guessed. No, but something sweet. The little men from Mainz were my favorite feature of local television: six cartoon characters whose three-second antics had been designed to distinguish public service programming from advertising, but they ended up enticing viewers to watch all the ads for fear of missing a moment of cuteness. I'd fallen in love with Berti and Det and their gnome-like buddies. When I went to graduate school, I tried to introduce the animated characters to an advertising class, but Americans weren't interested.

Eventually I asked Ingrid if we'd been singled out of that student crowd because my Indian dolls had caught her fancy. Or had John's use of his high school German charmed them? Human beings have a way of assuming the positive things that happen to them are due to some virtue or good deed of their own. In fact, Ingrid told us, we were favored by chance. As American students had begun entering and mingling in that social hall, they were intent on finding someone with whom they might speak English on a regular basis. How to choose? At some point, they decided they'd approach the very next couple to come through the door. *Bingo!*

I finally figured out what they wanted from us. Our friendship.

∾⫯∾

THE 'F' WORD

People never seem to want foreigners to know that their language has swear words. When I went to college, I had a roommate who lived in the Navajo Nation northeast of Flagstaff. As we shared duties at the home management house (a capstone requirement in a curriculum then known as home economics), Tallulah shared customs from her daily life: hanging sheepskin bedding outdoors and beating the bedbugs out of it, delaying baby showers until the birth of a baby to avoid bad luck. She taught us how to make Indian fry bread and brought in a traditional costume. She had me model it because she was seven months pregnant at the time. The dress was not the layers of gathered cotton skirt and rickrack I had expected but a slim-fitting, dark-red shift constructed of two woolen rectangles that might have been rugs had they been any thicker.

One morning, while Tallulah and another student were preparing refried beans and sunshine tacos (with scrambled eggs in the place of beef), the other girl burned herself in the kitchen, and we heard her swear.

"Would you believe there are no swear words in the Nava-way?" Tallulah asked us.

"You're kidding! Really? There aren't?"

Tallulah smiled her quiet smile. "Of course there are! Every language has bad words. I just said, 'Would you *believe* there aren't any?'"

Prior to moving overseas, the only naughty German word I knew was *arsch,* since John had once said it to a teacher in high school and gotten swatted on his. That word and one my father had picked up during World War II and pronounced "shizer."

We hadn't known Reinhardt and Ingrid long when I backed our sedan into a moving van and punched out a taillight. Where could I get this fixed? I asked. "Ah," Reinhardt replied. "You want to know what we know about fixing things? Well, I can tell you, we Germans invented the word." Ingrid shot him a stern glance. "*Ja,*" he continued. "Germans went to America, and they got trouble with mechanical things. The first time something broke down, they exclaimed, 'Fix it!'"

Again, a reproving look from his wife. "Reinhardt! *Genug.*" That's enough.

I smiled blandly and changed the subject, tucking the incident away in some corner of my mind, trying to figure out why Reinhardt was snickering about my accident.

Years later, an American attending an immersion program made it all clear to me. Bianca had visited her girlfriend Mari at the University of Marburg. Mari's wealthy boyfriend took them out to a fancy restaurant with his fraternity brothers, whose favorite sport was fencing. Seeking to make relevant small talk, Bianca asked the young man sitting next to her, "*Fickst du gern?*" instead of "*Fichst du gern?*" Rather than inquiring if he enjoyed sword fighting, it turned out she was propositioning him. And rather crudely at that.

When she related the story, an old memory struck me. I asked her, "Say that again. What are those two words?"

Then it hit me. "Fix it!"

I guess I'm a bit slow on the uptake. It took years for me to get the bilingual joke. *Touché,* Reinhardt.

~¡~

GERMANS MARCH TO PARIS. AGAIN.

The comfortably outfitted motorcoach left the hilly vineyard community of Bernkastel-Kues at 6 a.m., heading for Paris. By 6:50 a.m., our tour guides were passing around Mosel Riesling in real wine glasses. *Prost!*

The traveling group consisted of thirty-five Germans and two Americans. Fritz was to be our driver and tour guide. He was Ingrid's cousin, and he regularly did business in France. It was a privilege to be invited to accompany our new friends on one of Fritz's personally arranged trips. We'd gone to Paris with a busload of unruly soldiers. We'd visited the City of Light with my taxi-driving aunt. We'd never been to Paris with a bunch of Germans. This should give us another perspective on European travel.

The first destination was the Brasserie Löwenbräu on the Champs-Élysées. Three dozen Germans had traveled for five hours to go drink the most expensive German beer they'd ever bought.

When colleagues Mark and Millie had once refused to join us for a forty-course *rijsttafel* at the Indonesian Raden Mas near Amsterdam in favor of the McDonald's on Marktstraat, we'd decided they were typical gauche

Americans seeking the comfort of the known and the usual. Now our European companions were acting the same way.

That afternoon, in the adult-entertainment district of Place Pigalle, the bus got stuck trying to turn a corner. Fritz couldn't go forward, and he dared not back up. Men jumped off the bus to survey the situation. If only that little red car had parked a bit closer to the curb. One passenger got a gleam in his eye, and, the next thing we knew, four guys had picked up a Citroën deux-chevaux and scooted it over. *Voilà!* The merrymakers were underway again, but not before they got to ogle a few lingerie-clad ladies. For supposedly uninhibited Europeans, blasé about nudity and accustomed to topless beaches, these guys were as giddy and googly-eyed as any Midwestern teenaged boy has ever been.

That evening, a diner translated the French menu into English, and someone else translated that into German. One delicacy was described in especially flowery verbiage: *rognons de veau à la crème fraîche flambés au cognac.* It sounded quite elaborate: some kind of veal in a sauce prepared from thick, cultured cream and set aflame at your table with a splash of real Cognac. I didn't know what *rognons* meant, but if it came from a newborn calf, it was sure to be tender and juicy, and the sauce sounded marvelous. The waitress said she could not tell us which cut of beef or body part was *rognon;* she knew no other word or description for it. A butcher would normally use different terminology than is employed in medical references to anatomy. Where would it be on the human body? She couldn't say. Three men at the table decided to try it anyway. It was indeed sumptuous. John alone recognized the part of the calf that had been so carefully prepared. If the server had been trying a bit harder, she could have come up with a common French equivalent I would have recognized: *les reins*. Kidneys.

By the following evening, we had split into various interest groups, Reinhardt and Ingrid accompanying us to a tiny restaurant we had read about. We walked up the slopes to Montmartre and sought out an establishment once frequented by Picasso. The bistro had a television on one of its maroon walls but not a cubist reproduction in sight. The place was quaint, dimly lit, and quiet despite a few other customers seated at small tables against the opposite wall. The menu was larger than the establishment. It offered *plats du jour* (no, they don't call them entrées) like fish in white-wine sauce, pâté, and escargots in garlic butter. Desserts like *crème brûlée,* pineapple in kirsch, *pêches Melba,* and *profiteroles.*

Dinner was exquisitely prepared. Service was excruciatingly slow. By the end of the protracted evening, we realized that one Frenchwoman, *une femme d'un certain âge,* was doing all the cooking, serving the wine, and waiting on every one of the half-dozen tables in the establishment.

Across town, one of our travel mates had fared less well. He'd ordered beef too rare for his taste, so he summoned the waiter and asked if the chef might cook the meat a little more, *s'il vous plaît.* The waiter looked at the plate. He looked at the customer. Then he grabbed the diner's beer glass, poured its contents over the plate, gathered up the corners of the linen tablecloth, and vanished with the whole mess.

The weekend excursion took us to the avant-garde, wrong-side-out Centre Pompidou. To museums including the exquisite Jeu de Paume housing Impressionist paintings. We were close enough to touch (but don't you dare!) Whistler's Mother, Monet's fields of poppies, Gauguin's Tahitians, Degas' ballerinas, and Van Gogh's church in Auvers-sur-Oise. Of course we climbed the Eiffel Tower and drove around Place de l'Opéra.

At the flea market, some of our cohort bought what a French vendor had labeled an American sandwich: a hard roll sliced lengthwise, filled with two hotdog-like sausages, and topped with what we, but not he, would call french fries.

Our last stop was at the Arc de Triomphe. The Germans discussed the exaltation and humiliation of "Kaiser Napoleon," then surprised us by laying a wreath near the Tomb of the Unknown Soldier from World War I.

On the bus heading home, the driver's microphone was an irresistible attraction to several passengers who took turns singing songs, telling jokes, relating anecdotes, and describing one another in less-than-favorable light. *"Hier ist die Helga, die früher brünett war, jetzt aber blonde ist,"* meaning that the lady in question had recently ceased dyeing her gray hair. Helga blushed.

The two foreigners on board understood most of the jokes. All except the punchlines. We did then what we so often did during social repartee overseas: we sat there with silly grins on our faces. We'd laugh if we understood. Or because we didn't understand. Or simply because the laughter of other people was contagious.

~ ! ~

YOU REALLY LIVE HERE WHEN YOU START GOING TO WEDDINGS

Bells are ringing in the thirteenth-century Romanesque Cathedral on the marketplace this morning. Angelika and Charles are getting married in the church with the tall panes of stained glass. They're not the original Medieval windows; those were destroyed in an explosion, not during World War I or II but in a 1921 BASF fertilizer-plant explosion in Ludwigshafen, sixteen kilometers away.

Friends and family gather before the wedding at the bride's parents' house. She looks radiant in layers of white lace pinned in tiers with tiny pink bows. A gossamer ribbon streams over her dark curls and down her back. She carries a floral bouquet, but she won't be tossing it away to some bridesmaid. That is not a German tradition.

The groom, with his American family, is at the house too. There is no taboo against his seeing the bride, much less the dress, before the ceremony. His mother wears a pink brocade sheath and pink pumps with a chunky heel. Her mother wears a white skirt and black silk blouse. It's elegant, and the color choice is not as a testimony against the groom. She quite likes him because he's an officer, he's learning German quickly, he has a sense of humor, and he adores her daughter.

Shiny, clean cars wend their way through village and vineyard, their horns honking, with white streamers fluttering from their antennas. We are in the procession too, honored to be part of a private local event. We've known the bride since she was fourteen.

Inside the high-ceilinged chapel, it's cool and dim. Loved ones, who have watched this romance develop, now listen as Angelika and Charles repeat vows that sound all the more solemn for their Teutonic unfamiliarity. We don't understand what's being said. Neither do the groom's parents. No one is available to translate for them.

The groom presents his bride with a plain gold band. Though he could afford it, he has not offered his bride a diamond ring. She does not seem to expect it. I think he should do it anyway, if this is to be a bicultural alliance.

Outside in the sunshine, the bride's girlfriends suppress giggles as they string up a makeshift clothesline and drape it with dishtowels and baby clothes. In a moment, the unsuspecting groom is assailed, and the dress-blue uniform of a U.S. Army officer is covered with a frilly, pink apron. He is not permitted to remove it until he has taken all the "laundry" off the line. He is a good sport about it.

Horns honk as the party proceeds to a restaurant for the reception. In the courtyard, the couple greet their guests. Bubbling *sekt* is served to complement a formidable array of cakes and tortes, most of them baked by the bride's mother and aunts. *Linzertorte* full of hazelnuts. *Bienenstich* rich with honey. *Pflaumenkuchen* topped with halved plums. Strawberry torte. Cherry pie with pits still in the fruits. Black Forest chocolate. Coconut, cherry, every flavor of fresh fruit. There is no three-tiered cake with gritty Crisco icing (thank heaven for small favors). These colorful, homemade treats are infinitely tastier.

This is only the beginning of the feast. In the evening, a lavish meal will be served in courses to guests who are seated according to carefully arranged place cards. We will sit with the bride's uncle who, like I, speaks French. In the intervening hours, guests may mingle indoors or out, meet the families, chat with grandmothers over tea, or stroll along a nearby stream. The bride's mother has changed to another nice outfit and comfortable shoes. The groom's mother can't get back to her hotel, so she is stuck wearing her pink dress and heels all day and night. We go for a walk with her so she has someone to speak English to. The bride will not change her dress because she loves the way it looks and feels, and she knows she won't wear it again.

At dinnertime, we reconvene. Dancing, laughter, and wine will mingle late into the evening, and the bride and groom will remain for most of the party. Their wedding trip may begin in the morning, but tonight the newlyweds graciously attend to their well-wishers. In the USA, relatives may travel halfway across the country to attend a ceremony on an occasion so hectic they can barely exchange an uninterrupted sentence with the bride or groom. This German practice was more gracious than the way American couples traditionally left the premises before the end of the reception.

Earlier in the week, the civil ceremony that is the legal counterpart to this day's religious commitment was held in town. Only immediate family attended. The weekend before that was a *polterabend,* a casual sort of co-ed bridal shower. We were invited to that too. It was for friends of varying degrees of acquaintanceship such as colleagues and neighbors. There I met a man who had invented the dripless laundry detergent cap. I said it was nice to see him and that we could talk more at the wedding reception, unaware that the two guestlists were not overlapping and I would not see him again.

You have to invite your neighbors to the *polterabend.* They'd know it was going on anyway by the sound of breaking pottery. Each guest brings a piece of porcelain to smash at the entrance. This gesture announces his arrival and brings good luck to the betrothed. Some people go out and buy a stack of cheap dishes to shatter. Occasionally a couple of pranksters have the audacity to lug in an old toilet. After all, that's porcelain too. The bride's father indelicately pointed out that my charming Naïf dinnerware was manufactured by Villeroy and Boch, a major brand name in porcelain bathroom fixtures. The happy mess gives guests a chance to judge how compatibly the new couple share in the sweeping up. In this case, the bride's father did the cleanup by himself the next morning. I hoped that this wouldn't bring them bad luck.

Most Americans come and go as military occupiers or tourists. They don't get this backstage glimpse of the culture in their host nation. Once you have friends close enough to invite you to family rituals, you can really say you live there. It doesn't exactly make you an expatriate, but you begin to feel more like you belong.

BILINGUAL MARRIAGE

It is sometimes said that the partner who controls the bank account holds the power in a marriage. In a bicultural relationship, it could be said that the power belongs to the person who gets to speak his or her own language the most.

Encountering international cultures is exciting and enriching. It can also be exhausting. The simplest of everyday interactions is complicated by its need to be transacted in the local tongue. It's not hard to buy an item you see in a store without speaking English. It's relatively easy to conduct the routine transactions of running a household without a strong command of your spouse's dialect: clean and cook and dress the baby. It's more complicated when you need to have something replaced or repaired. Harder yet to explain how you felt about your childhood experiences or why certain things make you really mad or sad.

The language of the heart is the language one uses to count, pray, and swear, a linguistics professor once told me. In an intimate relationship involving two languages, he said, someone has to say or hear "I love you" in words other than those he grew up associating with mankind's most profound emotion. It's true: If a handsome man were to confide to me, *"Ich liebe dich,"* I'd have to recover from laughing before I could respond. The phrase sounds gruff at best and obscene at worst.

In the best mixed-language unions, each partner makes an effort to learn the other's native tongue, regardless of where they make their home. Some couples work out unique codes, linguistic combinations that switch back and forth mid-sentence. Maybe even mid-word. They make up verbs, combining English stems with German prefixes.

"Hast du dein Auto ge-polished?"

"Nein, ich war too busy."

They might develop a hybrid syntax.

"Where are, then, your shoes, young man?"

They may get overly literal.

"Das macht sinn." Which means, word-for-word, "That makes sense." Except that it doesn't make sense so say it that way to a Bavarian, who would expect to hear, *"Das ist aber logisch."* That's just logical.

While scholars of either language may cringe, these couples understand one another quite well. They amuse themselves with the linguistic combinations they invent. Consciously or not, each is developing a growing vocabulary and grammatical ability in the other's language. Listening to their communication, one is reminded of twins who sometimes invent a "twin speak" comprehensible only to themselves. Somewhere down the line, if these linguistically "mixed marriages" result in offspring, their mixed coding may present problems. For now, it's a workable means of meeting a loved one halfway.

❧ ⸙ ☙

ALPHA MALE IN PRESCHOOL

When her daughter announced she was expecting a son, Oma was as proud as any grandmother. She set up a nursery at her house, outfitting it with handmade quilts, Mickey Mouse linens, Winnie the Pooh baby clothes, and soft toys so he could comfortably spend time there. After his birth, she made his baby food and cuddled him and murmured to him in German. She took pictures of his doing perfectly ordinary activities and showed them off at any opportunity. There were even videos of his having his diaper changed.

When he began to walk, I had the pleasure of accompanying Oma and Carlo on a short stroll in the forest. The toddler would pick up a rock here or there, discarding this one for that more interesting one. Oma inquired what the little guy planned to do with his newest treasure, *der Stein.*

"Rock," Carlo said.

"*Ja, Stein,*" Oma repeated.

"*Du, Stein.* Papa, rock," he explained. "I/we, rock."

That was how he had come to refer to himself: I/we. Carlo was growing up in a bilingual setting and, while it's an enviable opportunity, it can take longer to sort things out. Mama and grandparents spoke German to him at home. His American father addressed him in English.

Sometimes what came out of his own mouth was a mashup. Confused by sentences that were so different and words that were so similar, he developed his own style. *Apfelsaft* became not apple juice but "poppysop."

Perhaps preschool would help, his parents thought. He'd hear one language all day long from fifteen or twenty peers. Although the teacher understood the goal, she was powerless to control what happened next. Within days, all the children waiting for a snack were asking for biscuits and poppysop. Carlo had become the alpha male of his preschool.

He could charm everyone from three to ninety-three.

"Ach! Du, mein kleiner Lilliput! Weißt du eigentlich wie sehr ich dich liebe?" Oma exclaimed, lifting him high into the air. "Do you have any idea how much I love you?"

A couple of years later, when it was time for first grade, Carlo's mother explained to the teacher that he was bilingual, which might affect his speaking or writing. After a few weeks of school, the boy came home distressed one afternoon. His teacher had asked him to translate an Italian phrase for his German classmates. He'd been embarrassed and at a loss as to how to comply.

"Why would she think I speak Italian?" he asked his mom.

"Ach so! It must be because of your name." She had not thought to specify that Carlo's second language was English.

❧ ! ☙

177

POLYGROK

BABY TALK FOR GROWNUPS

Justin, at a sophisticated four years of age, was fascinated to hear his parents pronounce words the way he used to baby talk them when he was a less erudite two years old. Appoo meant apple. Biboo was the yellow Sesame Street character (who one day flew out of the car window). Manonoos was McDonald's, which every kid clamors for, whether he'll actually eat his sandwich or not. We learned that watoo meant horse and about the anatomy of the family dog, Ranger: "Wanjer have nippoos." Justin was so caught up in the game of meeting his former linguistic self that he began to ask his mother for "Baby Dustin" words for everything. "How did I say, 'refrigerator'? How did I say, 'eat'? How did I say, 'Play with clay'?"

Mom had to explain to him, then, that his former speech pattern was a matter of a few mispronunciations and not a whole different language.

Some students in our Gateway classes approached their study in a Justin-like manner. They conceived of sentences as precise equations wherein each term in their native tongue must have a counterpart expression in the target language. When word-for-word translations were not presented, their equations did not balance.

Unfortunately, languages don't work that way. While sentences do have a mathematical aspect, word-for-word mindsets will not get you from our, "I like it!" to the more-common conventions which are formed something like, "It pleases me." One would never seriously interpret the French, *"qu'est-ce que c'est?"* as, "What is it that it is?"

A teenager we met in Mannheim inquired at what age American youths were legally deemed adults. He was incredulous that we could not tell him our word for this coming-of-age birthday, a term that would equate to his *volljährigkeit*. Full-yearly-ness.

The Germans, it seems, have a word for everything. Of course they do. They can make up new ones anytime by stringing together an entire sentence's worth of extant terms.

Even knowing that German was the language of such sophisticated thinkers as Kant, Heidegger, Habermas, Schopenhauer, and Schweitzer, I teased our friend about it.

"Actually, there are only about two hundred real words in your language," I told Reinhardt one day. "The rest of it is composed of combinations and permutations of that basic list. Our language is more sophisticated, because you have to study Greek and Latin to learn the origins of English words."

We use syllables like -ology, pre-, exo-, homo-, pneu-, mort-. Combining these imports from extinct languages makes us sound refined. Deutsch, however, combines its own little words ad infinitum. Naturally it's going to sound like baby talk. Consider these examples:

Spiel+zeug=play thing (toy).

Werk+zeug=work thing (tool).

Flug+zeug=flight thing (airplane).

Here's a personal favorite: *stink+tier*=stink animal (skunk). A child, having a limited vocabulary, would make up a word like that. Or this one, meaning glove: *handschuh*, literally a shoe for your hand.

The list goes on:

Schleim+haut=slime skin (mucous membranes).

Staub+sauger=dust sucker (vacuum cleaner).

Glüh+birne=glowing pear (a light bulb).

Achtung! It gets worse.

Das scham+haar=shame hair (pubic hair). The average German (I know; I asked an average German) does not consciously think of "shame" when he says this compound word. For him it's a gestalt.

Of course, we do some of the same thing in English. It's just not as funny when we do it. Voice box = larynx. The white of an egg is an egg white. But for the yolk we don't say "egg yellow," so when they say it *(eigelb)*, that sounds made up.

The fact that German is baby talk doesn't mean it's easy. You are aware of this if you've ever tried to carry on a conversation with a fifteen-month-old. Sometimes the compound nouns added up don't equal the sum of the parts. How many people would instantly recognize *sauerstoff* (that which acidifies things) as oxygen? Unless you're aware of the eighteenth-century idea that oxygen was a necessary ingredient in all things acid. Which was actually a pretty sophisticated notion in its time.

COMPUTER TRAINING IN GERMAN(Y)

It's hard enough to learn a computer system without doing it in a foreign language. This was the challenge faced by American users of CompuGraphic typesetting equipment in Germany.

The training site was in a village between Frankfurt and Darmstadt. There I spent two weeks wrestling with three strange concepts: computer jargon, metric measurement, and German explanations mixed with English terminology.

You can't blend into the crowd when you enter the classroom and the nameplate on your desk immediately identifies you as "Mrs." whereas the other students have *Herr* or *Frau* or *Fräulein* before their surnames.

I'd been studying and practicing regularly in social situations. There remained, however, conversations in which I got completely lost. When that happened, it was usually possible to get by with nodding and smiling. In a larger group, I could simply bow out of the conversation for a while, unnoticed, until something I understood penetrated my reverie and prompted me to contribute.

Not so in the class expertly taught by Frau Blass. *"Haben Sie verstanden? Sind Sie sicher?"* She was thorough and persistent. "Are you sure you have understood everything so far? If not, we can go over it again. This concept is important." No faking it here. No way to evade the instructor's penetrating gaze. When she saw that I did not understand, how could I indicate what I was not getting: her German or the software function? The medium or the message?

The class grappled for hours with millimeters, U.S. publishers' pica points, and the European system's ciceros. Our little international gathering labored to memorize computer codes that had been named in English by an American manufacturer and conveyed in German by a lecturer and lesson book. While I was figuring out that *wortzwischenraum* meant simply "space between words," my peers were thinking up ways to remember ALD, advanced leading, and FP, forward point. Together they'd devise *eselsbrücken*, donkey bridges, their idiom for mnemonic devices.

When evening came, I'd return to my hotel exhausted without having exerted a major muscle group all day. Perhaps a review of my notes would help shuffle the pieces into place? No, Frau Blass insisted we must relax at night, and that she would lead us in a thorough review in the morning. Sometimes I'd go with a fellow student to one of the restaurants in town. There were three to choose from: *Zum Eulchen, Gasthaus zum Lämmchen,* and *Das Zwiebelchen.* As my classmate pointed out, their names all featured diminutives: the little owl, the little lamb, the little onion.

In the morning, we'd start typing again. When a code was mis-entered, the PowerView 10 would *pip,* as my fellow students called it, tattling to the rest of the class that you'd made an error. I began to talk quietly to my terminal, personifying it, imploring its cooperation. My comrades did likewise, cajoling the system with *"Hallo! Du da, Junge!"* Hey, listen here, kid, do as I meant, not as I said.

From the first exercise, I realized that the German keyboard was laid out differently than the American. Most notably, *y* and *z* had switched places when nobody was looking. Those letters occur more commonly than you might think. By the end of the course, I was growing used to the alternate placement, just in time to go home and readjust. My classmates, meanwhile, had to get used to the idea that "O" stood for "On" with the U.S.-made system. They were used to graphic symbols with a short, vertical line representing the flow of current and a circle meaning the circuit was interrupted. "O" meant "Off."

For those ten days, as for the previous few years, I listened to Germans constructing sentences with verbs left until the end. It seemed so backward. Amusing, then, to hear a corresponding accusation: "Why does 'scroll down' take you to the top of the text?" Frau Blass asked the class in review. "I don't know," Frau Schacht ventured. "Maybe because English is so turned around?"

When our teacher sensed our frustration building too high, she announced a *kaffeepause* and distributed chocolate-covered cookies "for the nerves" or shared some comic relief: photocopied cartoons with the same sort of office humor one would encounter in a civil service setting. For example, a computer operator clutching the plug to his computer and boasting to a colleague, "He's a lot more cooperative since I explained to him that his life is hanging by a cord."

By the end of the course, we had been exposed to all of the code and format possibilities the typesetting system offered. We had tried each one for ourselves at least once. *Schritt für Schritt.* One step at a time. And something else: We had become friends. German and American. Human and machine.

TOO FLUENT TO UNDERSTAND

When an American says he understands more German – or French or Spanish or Italian – than he speaks, I'm sometimes skeptical. After we'd been overseas a year or so, John and I found the opposite to be true. We'd gotten to the point in our language development where we were able to express ourselves on almost any topic necessary for day-to-day survival. Given enough time and a patient listener, we could eventually spit out something close to what we intended. The difficulty came when one of our more-practiced questions yielded a too-fluent response. Well-turned phrases reap fluent answers, and rapid-fire responses can lose the neophyte in a hurry.

Those who say they can read more German than they can catch aurally are most likely correct. Reading can be done slowly and is free of accent or dialect. Spellings offer intelligible hints at friendly cognates.

When I was a child, my mother had a French acquaintance who babysat the neighbor's children. Simone spoke only the English she had been taught by GIs during the war. Her usage had not benefited from formal education or ample opportunity to practice. She had endless ways of butchering English. She'd urge her babysitting charges, "Eat your plate." When friends promised to visit her, she enthused, "I see you coming!"

English is difficult to master, my mother told her.

"*Ah, mais non*," Simone insisted. "*Bah alors*, I don't read eet or write eet, but to speak eet eez eezy!"

Without reading the languages I've studied, I would never have achieved any level of fluency. And that includes English. Being visually minded, I've always had to know the spelling of a word before it would stick in my mind. If I meet a girl named Cathy, my first question is, "*C* or *K*?" I have to know where to file her. When someone tells me a new word, I have her spell it for me. That way it's recorded in my mind's eye, and I can fast-forward to the right spot the next time I need it.

If I'm not in a position to capture the orthography of new vocabulary, I'll mentally assign it a phonetic spelling. This method can occasionally backfire. My freshman-year French teacher believed in immersion and conducted the class almost entirely in French. *Vive le français!* We could usually get the gist of what she was saying, and she would resort to English explanations only when truly necessary.

The first phrase she taught us was, "*Puis-je parler anglais?*" asking permission to switch to English. More often than not, she said *non*, insisting we noodle over the problem a bit longer. Some words she used never appeared in our reading, so I'd make up a spelling. When the teacher needed to explain a vocabulary term, she'd say words that sounded like "sa vedire." I concluded there must be a French verb "vedire" that meant "to mean," though I couldn't find it in the *Petit Larousse* that Mémé had sent to my older brother years earlier. It was the end of the school year before I realized she was saying, "*Ça veut-dire.*" It wants to say.

❧

FURTHER ABROAD

LOST IN TRANSITION

"**A** person never starved to death by getting lost," Aunt Charlene said. She's probably right, though personally I try never to say never. My high school drama director taught me that, and life has since proven its wisdom. Anyway, hunger was not the discomfort that worried me when I got behind the steering wheel. It was anxiety. Fear of getting lost felt nearly as bad as actually being lost. So great was my self-doubt that merely listening to directions on how to get somewhere could initiate a panic attack.

No matter where you were in town, an American would give you directions from the *kaserne*.

"It's four blocks west of the main gate."

"OK, when you leave the barracks, turn right and go under the tunnel, then take a right..."

"Drive around the base, and continue until you can turn left onto the Nibelungen Bridge..."

It didn't matter if you were in Rheindürkheim 8 kilometers north of town, trying to find the Alter Gasthof in Ibersheim 17 kilometers north of town, the directions would reference the army base a stone's throw away from the town center.

"In Germany, there are always at least two ways to get there," John liked to say, "but neither is clearly superior." If he could think of two ways to reach a place, I could generally find at least three ways to get lost. If I missed a step, I couldn't count on making three right turns to get back to my intended intersection. European cities are rarely laid out on a grid with junctions at neat, ninety-degree angles. When I did encounter such a layout, the street I wanted to take was usually a one-way road. Going the other way.

Multiply the speeds by three and the anxiety by six, and you have the *autobahn*. The keys to success on the *bundesautobahn* system are having a good sense of direction and a sound mental image of the geography. Neither of which did I have.

Even if you're a reasonably good map reader, and I wasn't, you have to plot your path in advance. Changing lanes on the autobahn is like trying to parallel park when all the cars, including yours, are moving at 100 mph. You can't be consulting a map and making last-second decisions on the fly.

German governments are masters at signage. (I've heard tour bus drivers curse the French for not being equally precise.). A plethora of notices and instructions have been posted to show the way. However, they're whizzing by at 160 kilometers per hour, obscured by a right lane full of 18-wheelers, and if you don't know the relationships between the major cities referenced and your desired destination (which is not listed on the sign), the information is of little avail.

For example, if you want to reach the famous but small city of Worms from Mannheim, you don't head for the nearest autobahn expecting to see the name Worms posted every 10 km in between. You might need to know that Worms is north of Mannheim, and that both of them are between Frankfurt and Stuttgart. But which direction would they be on a compass? While negotiating all this, you don't dare ride in the far-left lane because you can't compete with Mercedes and BMWs trying to blow you off the road, not with honking horns but with flashing headlights. You don't want to stay in the far-right lane tucked in between semi-trailer trucks twice your width and thrice your height; they're lumbering along at 50 mph and blocking your view. So you land in a middle lane with high-speed traffic on both sides of you. At the right moment, you need to return to the rightmost lane to take the northbound off-ramp. Just as you enter it, slowing down, a Beamer looms from behind, accelerating. He has come from the southbound on-ramp that shares one curve of pavement, and he wants to change lanes with you, preferably not at the same instant.

A trip to the Rhein-Neckar shopping center in Viernheim would take most drivers half an hour. You leave Taukkunen Barracks, take highway A6 heading west, get on the B9 going north, loop around, turn left, and you should be there. Unless you're navigationally challenged. It took me hours of traffic, turns, second-guessing, panic attacks, and petrol use before I got there. Even then I couldn't be particularly proud of my accomplishment because, when I finally stumbled on it, the mall was on my left, and I'd expected it to appear on my right.

One of my road trips was intended to be a quick after-work errand to pick up a farewell gift for a secretary. My objective was to purchase a piece of Wedgwood to add to her collection. "I wonder why women like little boxes so much," she'd once commented. "Maybe it's because we have wombs."

Knowing my proclivity for getting lost, Millie offered to go with me. We made it to the Mannheim PX but got confused returning to Worms. Probably chattering and not paying attention.

"I know we're on the right road," Millie insisted. "We're just heading the wrong way."

She was right. We were unwittingly en route to Basel, Switzerland. I had meant to take an exit off the autobahn, but had mistakenly entered a *kreuz* that took us onto another autobahn, leading us on a high-speed tangent to parts unknown. We were lost, in danger of being late for the going-away banquet. In a panic, I took the next exit, and we started looking for a payphone to call our husbands' office.

"We're lost. Come and get us! We have no idea where we are."

I was yelling into a pay phone in a mustard-yellow DBP booth in some village, and all I could tell John was that it was a town with a police station that was closed, a streetcar that had almost run me over, and churches whose bells were preventing me from hearing him clearly. It was like the woman in the joke who called her husband for help finding her way to her home somewhere in Deutschland. He asked what part of town she was in, so she glanced out the phone-booth door and announced that she was at the intersection of *umleitung* and *einbahnstraße*. Detour and One Way Street, two of the country's most common signs.

Click. Our line went dead. More money into the slot. I tried again. This time John couldn't hear me at all and hung up. I was using Millie's last coins. Mark answered.

"Don't hang up! Don't hang up," we implored, but the black rotary phones at their army desks gave them no indication that anyone was on the other end of the line. They hung up. This was the second phone we'd tried, and we'd used our last 10-*pfennig stück*.

Finally, we came upon an open petrol station and asked an attendant for directions. Now we were lacking words, not coins. But our plight was obvious, and he made himself understood.

We got back barely in time for the party, but if I wanted to return and thank the helpful man at the gas station, I could never find him again.

It was some comfort to me that occasionally I'd see a car with local license plates pulled off to the side of a road, brake lights on, the driver unfolding a huge paper map across the dashboard.

Ach so! You don't have to be a foreigner to get lost here.

⁓ I ⁓

LOOKING AT CLOUDS FROM BOTH SIDES

No one knew Paris better than Aunt Muriel. She was, after all, a *chauffeur de taxi* there for twenty-five back-straining years. She could negotiate all the grand boulevards, change lanes in traffic circles, find every diagonal warren in any *arrondissement*. She didn't have her own car, though, and, if we used her taxi for touring the countryside, we'd have to pay mileage to the G7. When we took the train to France to visit her, she decided it might be a good idea to borrow a friend's vehicle and proposed we go have a look at it.

Muriel never left the house early unless it was to meet someone at a train station, so John took off on his solo sightseeing tour in the morning, wanting to walk in the Bois de Boulogne at leisure. Muriel suggested he meet us at two o'clock at Porte de Saint-Cloud.

After two Metro rides and two short walks, Muriel and I arrived at her friend's place. He was not home, but we found his tiny orange car, a British model with the steering wheel on the right and an unfamiliar gearshift. Without trying it, Muriel announced, "I 'ave no idee 'ow to drive such a zing."

John hadn't shown up, and Muriel surmised we might be having a failed rendezvous. Ah, maybe he went to Pont de Saint-Cloud, she thought. It was a forty-minute walk between the two, so Muriel went around a corner and hailed a taxi to take us from Porte de Saint-Cloud to Pont de Saint-Cloud.

Meanwhile, at the west end of the bridge, John had unfolded his Paris Falk Plan to study the possibilities. That's when he realized there were two similarly named destinations: Porte de Saint-Cloud and Pont de Saint-Cloud. Vexing French language, he mused; they must be at the other one. An elderly Frenchwoman was alone at a bus stop with a cloth grocery sack, frilly green lettuce and a crusty golden baguette sticking out of it, and he summoned his well rehearsed phrase, *"Pardon madame, je voudrais aller..."* Using the international language of signs and smiles and pointing at a map, the woman identified the number line that would take him to us. He pulled a bright-yellow carnet from his pocket and took the recommended autobus. He arrived at the *porte*. No Muriel.

Muriel and I got to the west end of the *pont* by taxi. No John. The driver turned around.

John started walking back along the *pont*. This time we noticed him on the footpath by the bridge, and we leaned out the window calling wildly to him.

Finally, we were reunited. Muriel explained the difference between *pont*, which means bridge, and *porte*, which means gateway. John complained that, when you speak through your nose, they sound the same, and why hadn't I translated thoroughly? Or enunciated better? It was hours later than we had planned, we'd paid unnecessary fares, and now Muriel declined to borrow the car we'd come looking for.

⌐I⌐

THEY BURIED THE LEAD

Roland was a wine connoisseur. A linguist. A travel expert. A whiz at his job. So educated, so refined. His entire cohort of former colleagues deferred to him. They had apparently done so ever since they'd met him several career moves earlier. When he hosted a wine-and-cheese tasting, we attended. When he elaborated on some German word's etymology, we listened. Roland was new to us, but the other guys all knew him. A dozen white men working for a minority-owned, Washington-based consulting firm, they shared previous Department of Defense connections that bordered on nepotism.

John and I didn't idolize Roland, but we were respectful. And desirous of bonding with this convivial group setting up shop in Heidelberg. So when he organized a trip to Munich, we signed up, along with the other couples. All the men and their wives went, while the children stayed home. Except for Roland: his wife stayed home, while his eldest daughter went on the train with us.

Having booked an entire train compartment to ourselves, we were able to begin the party right away. Food and beverages we'd all brought with us were soon shared generously. I'm not a heavy drinker (a little goes a long way), but I do like to be involved in what's going on. Since

I'm short, I need a vantage point for my observations. By the end of the evening, I found myself stretched out on a long, narrow luggage rack overlooking rows of upholstered seats and the aisle where our new friends were telling jokes, chatting, and dancing.

After we had checked into our rooms in Munich and gotten oriented in the famous Bavarian capital (taking the measure of the city), we all enjoyed a traditional dinner, and then went out for drinks. Several of us turned in early, but the serious revelers sought out a familiar *kneipe*. As the night went on, even heavier drinkers like Frankie and Denton meandered back from the pub to the hotel, but Roland persuaded John to step into one last establishment.

Now, John appreciates an adventure once in a while: scuba diving, downhill skiing, rappelling over cliffs. On a TDY trip to San Francisco early in his career, he had been intrigued at the prospect of accompanying a senior non-commissioned officer for a night in the Tenderloin. The mission was aborted when the NCO tripped over a vacant tree well on the sidewalk. He fell to his knees, facing John and groaning. A feeble wino, leaning against a wall, misinterpreted this sight and dropped his brown paper bag on the cement, splashing Ripple on everyone. The rest of the evening was spent in the emergency department of Letterman Army Hospital, where the officer was treated for cracked ribs and a broken ankle. John's telling of this story was incidentally corroborated years later when I overheard a man at a party telling of his misfortunes in the City by the Bay. "You're the one!" I interjected. "You're the one who fell in the hole." I started to laugh but quickly realized that he still didn't see any humor in it.

In the bar in Munich, the atmosphere was genial, and the waitresses were pretty and friendly. Extremely friendly. Two of these women found themselves remarkably attracted to the two male tourists. They wanted to sit and get better acquainted with the American men, have a drink with them. Not just any drink. It seemed they favored a certain type of *sekt*, a German version of Champagne. The women insisted this was the only beverage they liked. It was quite pricey, but what the heck. This was a special evening in the convivial city of Oktoberfest fame. Bring it on! One bottle, then another. The men were getting happier, and the women were getting nicer. Eventually, the fräuleins proposed a little trek upstairs with hints at further friendliness. Roland followed them. What the heck. Prostitution was not legal in Munich, so the biggest news of the night was going to be the hefty bar tab. John was learning what a hustle bar was. He'd had enough adventure and declared it was time to go. Roland refused to leave, and John staggered back to the hotel on his own. I had spent most of the night in a strange hotel room, adjacent to people I barely knew, alternating between worry and fury.

Our second day in Munich was to be a full day of sightseeing, entirely on foot. John was weary, but I showed him no mercy as he dragged his feet around the city. His wayward buddy had not appeared for breakfast, and his teenaged daughter didn't know where he was or what to think. His colleagues' wives looked after the girl, reassuring her and trying to find her father, putting off the inevitable phone call to alert her mother in Heidelberg.

When Frankie and Denton finally phoned Roland's wife to admit the group's predicament, she notified them somewhat crisply, "He's here. I was wondering how long it would take you to call me."

It seems our new acquaintance had blackouts when he drank alcohol. He had eventually wandered from the bar out into the street, unsure where he was, unaware of how he'd gotten there or with whom, and uncertain about what to do next. He had no hotel key. His wallet had no cash in it, but there was a ticket. A train ticket from Munich to Heidelberg. He staggered toward the *bahnhof* and managed to get home.

Meanwhile, Roland's longtime buddies chastised John for leading him astray and abandoning him in downtown Munich. "Don't you know he's an inveterate alcoholic?" they implored. Perhaps someone might have mentioned that a bit sooner.

෴

WHY WOMEN TAKE LONGER IN
THE BATHROOM

You may judge restaurants by their cuisine, service, or ambiance. I have always built in a grading factor for the cleanliness of the bathroom. If that's not sanitary, how can the kitchen be? If there's no soap for the patrons, do the cooks wash their hands?

One can rarely fault German dining establishments for their lavatories. The *gasthaus* may be in a building older than America, but the restroom will be modern and clean. If you can't find it, look for steps leading downstairs to the basement. The entire room will be covered with gleaming, patterned ceramic tile that's color-coordinated to match the porcelains fixtures. A lot of avocado green in that era.

The potties are distinctive for their minimal use of water. There's a pipe leading into the toilet but no visible reserve tank. In the place of a bowl of water, there's a shelf. This is handy, by the way, if you need to obtain a stool sample for your gastroenterologist after you've contracted parasites in Egypt. Not very subtle, but ecologists like it because it uses so little water.

The facilities were peculiar but not primitive. The plumbing technology was, in fact, far more advanced than anything I'd encountered in America at that time. Warm-air hand dryers in the U.S. paled in comparison to the state of continental technology. Stopping at an autobahn restaurant on the way to Belgium, I could not figure out how to wash my hands after using the WC. There were basins with spigots but no hot or cold valves. No handles at all. The place was doing a fair amount of business (so to speak), so I decided to wait and study how other women managed to make the water flow over their hands. Minutes passed while women came and went without demonstrating the sophisticated equipment. Considering how many people failed to wash their hands, I was hoping none of them worked in this restaurant.

Apparently, someone outside was catching a glimpse of me whenever the bathroom door opened. Finally, the door swung open extra wide and a male voice called in, "Wave your hands! Wave your hands under the spigot!" It was my devoted husband, who had been catching sight of my puzzled countenance in a mirror every time the door opened.

I stuck one hand under the faucet, wiggled my fingers, and splash! Out came water. Activated by radar? Magic? Sensor faucets were not an American innovation.

Wow! Impressive ingenuity. What'll they think of next? I soon found out at a roadside stop near Spangdahlem, where the toilets had no knob, handle, or chain for flushing. There had to be a trick to it. What was I not seeing? Well, I shouldn't keep John waiting any longer, and I was only leaving a few drops of urine. Heck with it. "It's not my fault. It'll just have to flush itself."

It did. *Whoosh!* As soon as I unlocked the door.

⌐I⌐

ADVENTURES WITHOUT PASSPORTS

It was essential to show identity papers every time you crossed a national border. From Germany to France to Switzerland to Italy. Well, maybe not Italy; John once traveled to Venice without his passport.

Somehow, when packing for an official trip to Italy, he grabbed my passport instead of his own. This little distinction escaped notice when he left the Frankfurt airport, but it was a bit of a problem when he arrived at Venice Airport Marco Polo, and an Italian official compared the bearded man before him with the long-haired woman in the picture.

"*Questo non è il tuo passaporto,*" the man in the uniform said. This is not your passport. John explained in English that he did, in fact, possess a valid document but that he had mistakenly brought his wife's. See? Same last name.

"Si. Where isa' you passaporto?" Again, this is my wife's; I forgot my own. I'm sorry. Can we call her? I have other ID with me: U.S. military, my driver license. The official is nodding as the story goes on, as though he's following every word. But at the end of the second explanation, and the third, the response is still, "Yes, but where is your

211

passaporto?" Finally, the official sighed and motioned for John to proceed to baggage claim and into the country.

Leaving Italy would not be a problem either, but it was doubtful he could talk his way back into Germany without proper papers. He had me meet him at the Frankfurt airport immigration desk so we could have the correct document passed along to the officials in passport control.

The trip to Italy had begun with a little bump when John, sitting at the departure gate, glanced at his ticket and read *Venedig* as the destination. "Venedig?" he exclaimed, dashing back to the woman at the Lufthansa counter. "I'm supposed to be going to Venice!"

The German agent, prim uniform, sleeked back hair, hollow cheeks, dead-eyed, weary voiced, informed John: "*Venedig* ist *Venice.*"

Having entered Italy more or less legally and much delayed, John finally picked up his rental car: a sleek and sporty little model. His first challenge was how to put it into reverse as he crept closer and closer to the concrete wall of the parking garage. It turns out, you squeezed up on a ring on the stick-shift knob. All right. He was on his way, braving the *autostrada,* where speed limit signs and lane markings were apparently mere suggestions, when it began to rain. Just a sprinkle. No problem. It was a warm afternoon, the windows had been left open, and the damp breeze was refreshing. Then it turned into an actual rain, and John thought he might roll up the window. Hmmm. No window handle, lever, knob, or button. Not beneath the window. Not on the door. Not on the dashboard. The shower became a downpour, and still he could not find a way to close the window. He hadn't reached his hotel, let alone started his job, and Italy seemed to be getting the better of him.

He rolled his eyes heavenward... and then he saw them. Two round buttons on the ceiling by the rearview mirror. The window controls.

The day had been a trying one. Dinner would be relaxing. He peeked at his Marling Menu Master but forgot to take it with him to the restaurant. That's OK, he could probably figure this out. How about a local specialty, a dish named in honor of this splendid city? He decided he'd try the *Fegato alla Veneziana*. Venetian-style something-or-other. Surely you couldn't get much more Italian than that.

Indeed, the meal was excellent. As long as you liked fried liver and onions.

ᶜ⌐ᶜ

ADVENTURES WITH LOSING PASSPORTS

"O Jerusalem, Jerusalem... how often I wanted to gather your children together, just as a hen gathers her brood under her wings, and you would not have it!" (Luke 13:34)

Mental preparation and appreciation can extend a short holiday. Anticipation and memories, bolstered by studying travel guides beforehand and reflecting on photographs afterward, can stretch the vacation experience and keep it memorable. Preparing to revel in Rome, I enrolled in an accelerated Italian course, bought lesson books, and listened to recorded lessons at the kitchen sink, the makeup vanity, and the steering wheel.

Viva Roma! Here we come.

It's only a three-day weekend, but we're going to have a great time. An easy time because we'll know our way around, be able to discern directions, and read historical signs and menus. We'll be welcomed by the locals who will appreciate our attempts to speak their native tongue.

It was after dark when we arrived. Before we could locate our shuttle bus, half a dozen taxi drivers descended on us, insisting on taking us to our hotel. A heavyset man with two days' beard growth and an electrolarynx assured us in metallic tones that the shuttle was not making any further runs that evening. It was too late. The tenacious band of chauffeurs for hire dogged us for half an hour, making pleas, proffers, and predictions until, lo and behold, our hotel shuttle arrived.

From our hotel window, the Colosseum was within sight. We found ourselves up looking at it several times in the night, trying to discern what the noise was all about. Someone was driving in circles on the deserted street and honking repeatedly for what seemed like hours.

In spite of that, we got up early because there was so much to see. So much walking to do in the City of Seven Hills. The morning meal was free, but there were no other guests in the breakfast room. We were energized as we dashed back upstairs to grab our daypacks. But where was my purse?

Two minutes. That's all it took for my belongings to vanish from the table and disappear into the pockets and trash cans of Rome.

I know, I know. I've heard it; I've even said it. Don't let your bag out of sight for a second. Don't dangle it by one hand on the sidewalk. Don't sling it casually over your shoulder on the subway. But I forgot. Excited about our plans for the next twelve hours, I let it slip my mind for just a moment. A minute that cost us most of a day.

The hotel staff denied any responsibility and referred me to the police. "You will get money," they assured me.

That seemed unlikely, but we were directed to a police station where I spent an hour listing all the contents of my purse. This was not the context in which I'd imagined practicing my newly acquired Italian vocabulary.

Among the valuables in my purse were passports. Both John's and mine. It took an hour to reach the embassy. We had to pay for replacement documents and go up the street to get official photos made. If you think the average passport picture is unflattering, you should see one taken when you're disgusted and miserable. And you have to live with that image until the expiration date.

Our mini vacation was flying past, so we had to put the incident behind us. Unfettered by worldly possessions, we set off to see the Forum. We were outside the historic, crumbling walls when a boy approached me with a cardboard sign handprinted with *Bisogno di soldi*. Yes, well, I haven't got any money left to give you. See: no purse. As this child was prancing insistently in front of me, a smaller figure approached from behind on my right. I whirled in time to keep him from reaching into my hip pocket. Waving my arms, I was trying to fend off four little hands while crying out to John, who had run ahead to buy tickets. Now the bigger boy was reaching inside my unzipped leather jacket, looking for the secret pocket he knew from experience would be there. The juvenile thieves were not deterred until John ran over and grabbed one of them and tossed him aside. He fell to ground, transforming suddenly from adept criminal into whimpering child. Across the street, an adult guardian was watching but did nothing to intervene.

If he wanted us to feel sorry, we did. Sorry that my memories of this day would be marred by events like this. Sorry that ragged urchins had to beg and steal from well-heeled shoppers and tourists. Sorry he didn't have a better life or prospects.

Huckster cabbies did not make the Colosseum less magnificent. Purse snatchers did not make the Piazza Navona less colorful. Pickpockets did not make the Forum less historically significant. They did somewhat diminish my enthusiasm for the Eternal City. A city I'd prepared myself to embrace.

MERCHANT MARINES IN TUSCANY

Camp Darby is a rustic lodge, we were told. It's an inexpensive getaway for American military communities, and it's convenient to Pisa, Carrara, Cinque Terre, and other Italian experiences.

Rustic lodge? It was an open field of grass with a string of slapdash cabins around it. Under the ill-fitting door, a one-inch strip of light shone; and other things came in that way too. From the bathroom, with its too-dark-blue enamel walls and asphalt-tile floor, came a rustling noise. The scratching sound issued from a three-foot-high metal cylinder, the kind of trash can one finds in public restrooms. A snake? Could a snake crawl into a container that tall?

"John!"

He started poking around in the trash with a clothes hanger, then tipped the can over. Out ran a gray mouse. Not a big, ugly rat. Just a nice, little mouse. He scurried outside through the gap under the door and into the field. Hopefully, he didn't encounter the fox whose sparkling eyes caught our attention far off in the darkness.

Hospitality courtesy of the U.S. Army. I'd thought it was called "Camp" Darby because it was an army base, not because its accommodations so resembled sleeping in a tent. But the price was right.

Convenience, Darby's secondary benefit, was questionable too. If you'd flown in and didn't have a rental car, you'd have to take a bus to get to Livorno, and a bus and a train to get into Pisa, as the camp was so remote. There was a shuttle, but it didn't run often. We dreaded the thought of driving in any large, crowded city, and we had already observed that Italian drivers had little respect for highway lane markers, if indeed there were any lanes. John sauntered over to the bus stop to check out the schedule of rides into Livorno. Two men were sitting on the bench under the shelter, waiting in the late-afternoon sunlight. When five minutes had passed and he was still chatting with them, I assumed he must know them. Maybe these men were stationed in Germany or he had met them on some previous tour of duty.

Finally, John came back to report. "That's Mike and Rick. They said the bus won't show for another hour, so I told them we'd give them a ride into town."

"You what? Do you know these guys?"

"No, they're just a couple of bored sailors. Looking for something to do. They seem to know their way around Livorno, so maybe they can give us the lay of the land."

Most of the time, I can't get John to make a phone call to friends, much less talk to strangers on the street. He acts like he's shy.

219

"Wanna call Jim and Mary and see if they can go to dinner tonight?"

"Nah. They might say no. You call 'em."

Once in a while, he surprises me. Usually at the wrong times. Some sort of Body Snatcher invades his form, imbuing him with his father's extroversion; next thing I know, he's out befriending strangers.

Mike and Rick were heading toward our cabin, and there didn't seem to be any graceful exit now, so Officer Friendly went to get the car, and I ran inside to grab my jacket. The sailors climbed into the back seat of our car, and I twisted around to introduce myself. Rick's hair was too long for a sailor's. Mike seemed too old to be in the U.S. Navy. He wanted to go to a particular bar downtown. To soak up Tuscan culture? In fact, he wanted to meet some buddies at an Irish pub.

"How long have you been in the service?" I asked.

"Oh, we're not in the military. We have base privileges because we're Merchant Marines."

Not U.S. Marines. Merchant Marines. I began to shoot optical daggers at my oblivious spouse. We weren't helping our brave men in uniform on their way to war in the Middle East. We were giving rides to hitchhikers. Something that Mother had always said never to do. Although she did it herself once...

Living an hour away from Mexico, we used to find it convenient, interesting – and affordable – to purchase goods and services on the other side of the border. Bread, summer dresses, liquor, Indian jewelry. Even orthodontic care. My hometown had no dentist specializing in braces when I was a kid so, because I had sucked my thumb, my mother was faced with driving me to Tucson or Nogales once a month to get my hard palate widened and my teeth straightened. Nogales was closer. Also, half the price. We used to go with our neighbors, Robin and her son. The two moms took turns driving us to see Dr. Eduardo Jimenez Badillo. A certificate in his waiting room indicated he had gone to school in the USA. The dental visits went on for a couple of years, but once Patrick's teeth were all straight, it was Mother and I making the trips. Just the two of us.

Except for the day Mother picked up the hitchhiker.

We left behind the faded Mexican houses, dusty streets, and sidewalks that were always wet but never clean. We passed steep hills where old women dressed in black climbed scores of outside stairs to their dwellings. I leaned back into pillows in the back seat, queasy after someone had spent an hour with his hands in my mouth. We were on the narrow, winding highway, driving in and out of sunlight, where cut rock faces allowed the road to be built and the deep shadows to fall. I sat up when Mother pulled off the road and stopped the car.

A man in a dark-green wool uniform came running up to our white Dodge Lancer. "He must be from Fort Huachuca," Mother said. "He looks like an officer." The soldier climbed into the front seat, grateful for the ride, and the adults chatted intermittently during the ninety-minute ride across Santa Cruz and Cochise Counties. I sat in the back quietly.

Never pick up hitchhikers.

At the main gate to Fort Huachuca, the man got out. Mother turned to me sternly and warned: "Don't say a word about this to your father. I don't know why I picked him up. He could have gotten that uniform anywhere."

Ten years later, here I was in another country giving rides to sailors who weren't in the U.S. Navy and who didn't even have uniforms.

Livorno's layout proved to be more complex than Mike had recalled. Curving, one-way streets complicated our attempts to locate the bar in question, and it was getting dark. After about three times around a wide, tree-lined piazza, I convinced John to stop at a *gelateria* for directions. Officer Friendly seemed to have disappeared, and it was up to me to try speaking Italian.

"*Per piacere,*" I approached the ice cream shopkeeper. "*Cerchiamo Irish Pub.*" My Italian generally consisted largely of French with an "o" on the end of every word, but I managed to find out where the bar was, and I had the presence of mind to ask how to get back to our little hut on the prairie. "*O! Campo Darbay!*" the proprietor exclaimed, reinforcing my notion that any phrase can be made into a Romance language. "*Sempre dritto!*" Straight ahead.

We got to the pub by driving down a narrow alley. It was wide enough only for one lane but allegedly accommodating two-way traffic and lined with parked cars on both sides. Alcohol was no longer permitted aboard the ship, Mike advised. Not since the Exxon Valdez disaster. So the men had worked up quite a thirst.

A dozen other sailors were in the pub that spring evening. Not a single one had a peg leg or a parrot on his shoulder. There wasn't a beer belly or an eyepatch among them. They were mostly twenty-ish years old, fresh-faced, clean-shaven, and polite. Their biggest problem seemed to be that they were not allowed into Italian discos unless they brought their own dance partners with them. A high barrier to entry. Rick was ready to leave before Mike and asked us for a ride home.

Not exactly home of course. Not *Campo Darbay* since he had no affiliation with the military. His home was the Cape Canso. His ship.

"*Sempre dritto.*" Our lodging for the night was straight ahead, but we were not heading in that direction. We were driving toward some deserted docks in the dark, in an unfamiliar city, transporting a stranger with no last name and no witnesses. *And my mother has no idea where I am.*

Never pick up strangers.

We left the cream-colored buildings and strings of white lights, the tree-lined piazza, the happy faces at sidewalk restaurants. We passed dim streets of empty offices with gray concrete edifices. Through industrial zones. Across a lonely road, under a slate sky. Toward the docks, a gloomy area even in broad daylight. Which this wasn't. Silhouettes of masts and hulls became vaguely distinguishable against a glum horizon.

"You can drive around the other side and park behind there." Rick indicated the far side of the hulking freighter.

Sure. Then he can dump our bodies into the Ligurian Sea.

The ship loomed over us. I'd never seen a vessel larger than a rowboat. Trains and boats and planes. This was why I'd left my hometown. Because I wanted to see the world.

"Wanna come on board?" Rick asked. "I'll give you a tour."

In a second, John was out of the car and climbing up metal steps on the side of the ship. She'd launched in 1964, but for eight years had been stored along the Mississippi Delta and recently pulled out in support of the Persian Gulf War. Now she was tasked with delivering materials to Saudi Arabia. When a speedy build-up was called for, the United States augmented its naval forces by sending commercial ships and sailors to the Persian Gulf or the Panama Canal Zone. The Cape Canso was the only private vessel to reach her delivery destination under her own power, but on the way back she stalled in the water and had to be towed. The crew was obliged to stop in the Mediterranean, waiting for parts to repair the boiler. It was hard to find replacements, Rick explained, and that was what had kept him and Mike and their mates in Livorno for days looking for diversion.

The Cape Canso was a classic, and John was intrigued. We passed through the hatch that stood open to the night air, a warm, oblong glow against gray metal and deep-blue sky. The interior was a maze of narrow passageways. It was obvious the old ship had been repainted recently. A clean coat of thick, pale-yellow enamel covered every inch of her rough and rugged surface. The kind of paint job that older, less-loved items got, where nails, hinges, metal trim, and rubber seals no longer stood out in contrast but were camouflaged by haste, like pancake makeup applied to pitted skin.

Rick showed us the captain's quarters, galley, engine room, and bridge. We saw the ship's compass, radar equipment, satellite telephone, and signal flags. He was as proud as we were curious. In the boiler room, I stood gazing at red and gray pipes while my husband asked Rick endless questions about the ship's cargo, crew, and capacities. Men sporting dungarees, old shirts, and two days' beard growth sat playing cards in the break room. The tiny recreation area had an exercise bike, a small television, and a collection of well worn VHS movies. Pastries, fruit, chips, and beverages were available for the taking. Rick grabbed an apple and chomped hungrily, a mouthful bulging his lean cheeks. "Want some?"

In his cabin, he showed us textbooks he was studying to help him achieve the rank of able-bodied seaman. While in high school, he'd sold fish, lobster, or whatever was bringing in the best prices onshore. Now he was operating booms and hoists and working at the endless painting and lubricating jobs that kept a ship operational and rust-free.

We saw the plastic-sealed NBC gear he was issued when the ship arrived at the Arabian Peninsula. He and his buddies never knew if they might need protection from nuclear/biological/chemical threats in the same way as their active-duty counterparts.

We sat on bunks while Rick told us about his travels and what had brought him here. He had worked at a lumber mill in Maine, and he'd been smitten with a local girl named Susie. He set about building her a log cabin in the woods. As he placed each beam and stud and joist, Rick imagined Susie would marry him and move into that custom-made cottage with him. He designed a nice kitchen with fine wooden cabinets and a window that overlooked a secluded pine forest.

But when the last nail was driven, Susie didn't want to live in the log cabin in the woods. And she didn't want to marry Rick.

Storm clouds were brewing over Iraq at that time, and Rick heard the call for strong, young men to reinvigorate the Merchant Marines. Mothballed cargo ships were being launched to shuttle supplies to American military forces behind the scenes. And so Rick escaped the sad surroundings that reminded him of Susie, lured by exotic ports of call and someone, something, that needed him when she didn't.

Proudly, he showed us photo albums that proved he'd visited Sicily. Skied steaming Mount Etna. Docked in Panama. Dined in Istanbul. He was living a classic boy's dream: run away from home, go off to sea, travel the world. And serve his country too.

"One of these days you'll meet another girl to share a home with, the right girl," I predicted. Rick's eyes took on a doubtful, far-away expression.

"Hey! Look at this!" He pulled a box from beneath his bunk. "I've bought all this stuff. It was real cheap. To send to my family back home." When he was able to visit, they received silver jewelry from Italy, carpets from Turkey, and T-shirts from the Suez Canal. "I'm not always there for the holidays, so they have Christmas whenever I get there."

As we were leaving, he gave us T-shirts and trinkets. Souvenirs by which to remember places we'd never seen. We returned to the dock the next day, hoping to reciprocate by bringing Rick a gift.

"Y'all need somethin'?" A gruff sailor seemed to find the conventional-looking couple and their dark-blue Camry out of place on the dock.

"We're looking for Rick."

"He went into town."

"Oh. He said he'd be here this afternoon."

"Yeah, well, he's kind of a space cowboy."

I left the gift and a note with our mailing address, but we never heard from Rick. The T-shirts were indeed rather cheap, but I wore mine a few times, thinking of our adventurous young friend. I'd have liked to see that log cabin he built in the woods.

෴

TRAVEL AFTER TERRORISM

We awoke at 6 a.m. to a woman screaming in our bedroom. Our alarm clock turned on the radio when the Armed Forces Network began its morning news report. It was December 21, 1988. Pan Am flight 103 had exploded, and an aggrieved mother was reacting in shock and horror.

Some 270 people died in the bombing, but the greatest share of attention has always gone to the 35 students who were returning from a semester in London with the Syracuse University semester-abroad program. At that time, I had no idea John and I would ever have a connection to S.U. That we would later attend graduate school there.

Families everywhere were calling one another to discuss their holiday flight plans under the shadow of this terrifying event. Most were able to say, *No, we flew a different day, took a different airline.* Not because they had any special insight. Just by chance.

Frankfurt International Airport the day after the crash. Would passengers in line be on edge? Would someone on the plane get hysterical the moment the passenger exit swung shut? Would some nervous person get sick to his stomach and set off a chain of demands for little, white bags? Or would the entire terminal be empty?

Some people probably altered their travel plans. Most, however, went ahead with whatever reservations they had made. They reasoned that the days immediately following a tragedy were the safest time to fly because security would be especially tight. They didn't believe an attack like that could succeed twice in the same week. Or they wanted to get home so badly they decided to take a chance, realizing that, in spite of the enormity of the recent horror, the odds of their failing to reach their destination safely were one in several million. Or, regardless of their religious or philosophical persuasions, today they would assert that they were fatalists, that if they were meant to die that day it would happen, one way or another.

My mother used to say she believed this: "It's written. The day you are born, it is already written when you will die." She didn't necessarily live as though she believed that, but it was a useful idea to draw upon when a particular death seemed especially incomprehensible.

The airport seemed to be conducting business as usual. Pan Am appeared to be handling baggage check-in with exceptional care. The hot, white light of a television camera focused on a window at the Pan Am counter. The entire section was cordoned off, and bags were being opened and inspected. Rather akin to locking the proverbial barn door...

Travelers were asked the usual round of questions: *Did you pack your own bags? Did anyone ask you to carry anything for him? Have your bags been unattended at any time since you left home?* And finally, *Do you understand why we are asking this?*

Yes, everyone understood quite well. No one got impatient. Nowhere in the airport was anyone shouting at a ticket agent, complaining about missed connections, overbookings, or misrouted luggage.

Passengers were requested to stop on the tarmac and verify which bags were theirs before they were loaded. For some reason, or no reason, I made a silly remark about the Swiss chocolates I was taking to relatives and how they were melting under a rare beam of sunshine.

"I don't care about my things. And I don't mind the delay. It's worth it," said a quiet voice next to me.

She was a young woman cuddling her baby close to her. "I'm not afraid to die. I've had a full life. But he deserves to live. If somebody bombed our plane, that would be my first thought: my baby. I'd be angry all the way down."

A full life? She was maybe twenty years old, much like the Syracuse students.

❧ ! ❧

TIGHTENING SECURITY

Under Threat Con C, two identity cards were required for access to military installations. Vehicles were subjected to trunk searches; they had their undercarriages examined with instruments designed like long-handled dental mirrors blown up to snow-shovel proportions. Guards paced the perimeters of enclosed compounds. Men and women in camouflage uniforms guarded city street corners around the clock. Military personnel showed up to office jobs looking like giant insects in miserably hot, confining NBC gear (nuclear, biological, chemical suits and gas masks). Soldiers with M-26 shotguns were perched atop buildings at shopping centers. I'd never felt safer walking to night school.

Threat Condition Charlie went into effect across Germany the day the Gulf War began.

Driving past military housing that morning, we saw entire families on the lawn in front of their apartments: soldiers scrambling into their fatigues, girls in bathrobes and curlers, children in their pajamas, babies and dogs running about. Everyone had been evacuated for a search of the premises following an anonymous warning. Perhaps it was a crank call, but it could have been the real thing, and you never knew for sure. Maybe it was a practice drill that allowed terrorists to observe our reactions and readiness. Usually it was just a nuisance.

Americans living outside of military housing were urged to take extra pains to park their cars in garages (rarely available) and to check every morning for signs of bombs planted in them. I was hesitant to comply as that action in itself would look pretty conspicuous. We regularly complained about how distinctive the U.S. military license plates were. Totally different shape and type font from the European ones. Easy for a terrorist to identify at a quick glance. On a winter morning, John scraped ice from his windshield and drove to work. An hour later, he was back home. A bomb threat was being taken seriously, and workers were not permitted to enter the *kaserne*.

Security considerations delayed postal services, though I'm sure my mother believed any lapses in correspondence were strictly my fault. The APO refused to handle packages because their contents were not easily verified. Inside the post office were giant posters of wanted terrorists operating in the area. We were all exposed to regular briefings on the various anti-American groups operating overseas. Some terrorist acts were obviously anti-personnel, while others supposedly sought to destroy property. Harming civilians could be bad P.R. for the cause, and only the more radical fringes were willing to risk that.

No one complained about the added security measures aside from a few local protestors. And maybe my mother. Volunteer groups – women mostly – organized efforts to provide refreshments for the guards: warm beverages and soup along with homemade snacks.

Some social events were canceled, whether out of concern or respect for the Middle East conflict. For the most part, people went about their usual lives. They could not afford to change plans every time they heard of a threat of terrorist attack. There were too many. People were constantly aware of it at some low level. Most were more cautious than fearful.

"You can't think about it too much," said a German woman married to an American soldier. "You can't live your life if you're afraid all the time."

⁓I⁓

GUESS WHO'S COMING TO MAKE DINNER

One of the best things about my father-in-law, Tom, was his childlike exuberance for life. One of the worst things about him was his childish insistence that others match his sense of urgency. The trouble with Tom's enthusiasm was that he couldn't sustain it.

Case in point: Tom and John were making a cross-country trip visiting friends, family, and tourist sites, while I was starting graduate school. Tom had a habit of waking up early, coaxing his son out of bed, then driving for about an hour before getting sleepy and asking him to take over. After three or four of these morning switch-offs, John lost patience and rather sharply advised his dad that, if he wanted to get up early and go, then he should do the driving. If he wanted John to drive in the mornings, then let him sleep in, after which he would happily take the wheel. The next morning, Tom was up early again. "Get up! Let's go!"

Again John dragged himself from bed. Tom began driving while John napped in the passenger seat. A jerking of the car startled him awake as Tom swerved off the pavement and back onto the highway.

"What happened?"

"I guess I'm more tired than I thought I was. I must have started to fall asleep."

"Well, why didn't you wake me up?"

"Because you said not to get you up early, then end up asking you to drive."

"Well, yeah, but not if you're going to get us both killed."

Tom had mistaken a potty break for time to start the day. The following morning he let John sleep in.

Whether retirement or widowhood or two cardiac bypass procedures brought out Tom's impulsive personality traits, I couldn't say. But we thought we'd better prepare for his arrival. To Tom-proof the house if possible.

We were never the best hosts. My father-in-law would come to town and complain that our refrigerator was empty. Even now, years later, if we come home from the store and load up the fridge with fresh meats, sandwich makings, salad fixings, and a selection of cheeses, or if there happens to be some leftover casserole in a glass dish and fresh fruit in a bowl on the counter, we say, *It's too bad Dad isn't here; he'd be so proud.* Anticipating his arrival in Heidelberg, we splurged at the commissary, deli, and bakery. That way, he could snack whenever he wanted. Or cook dinner, if he wanted. Lord help us.

Tom and his sister were the first people I ever met who read cookbooks. They didn't consult them or peruse them; they actually read them with the anticipation normally reserved for adventure novels.

When a person likes to eat, it's a blessing if he is also enthusiastic about shopping and cooking. Tom loved food, and he loved to cook. He would try any recipe, no matter how exotic and involved, no matter how much specialty shopping or preparation it entailed.

His kitchen exploits brought three-quarters of the pans, mixing bowls, and implements out of the cabinets. If you could stay out of his way until he was done, this was fine. But, as his heart weakened and his angina worsened, his energy tended to wane before the cleanup was done. "I'm tired," he would suddenly complain, a slight Kansas drawl creeping into his speech so that it sounded like, "Ahm tarred." By this time, every counter surface in the kitchen was covered with batter-smeared bowls and greasy pots, grimy spice jars and licked spatulas. He'd amble off to the living room for a nap in his La-Z-Boy recliner and a swig of Jim Beam.

During his bread-making phase, he explored sourdough techniques. Wanting to be authentic, he got some starter and was growing his own "mother" on the counter by the range. His wife complained about the odor, so he put a lid on it. By and by it exploded all over the kitchen.

On one of his health kicks, he decided we should be able to have our cake and protein too, so he consulted various recipes, combined, experimented, and concocted some biscuits he assured us we could consume guilt-free. He'd worked hard to make sure they contained all the wholesome muffin ingredients he could find: oats, bran, flaxseed, rye, brown rice syrup, molasses, alfalfa powder, protein powder, low-fat powdered milk, and, for good measure, some kind of vitamin mixture. They didn't look too bad, and I had a known weakness for carbohydrates. *OK, I'll try one.*

It was awful. Like cardboard except sour and too hard to chew let alone swallow. Murmuring something I hoped sounded ambiguous, I called upon my childhood experience with peas and fatty beef stew and salmon croquettes with tiny bones in them: I sneaked down the hall to the bathroom hoping to spit it into the toilet and dispose of it quickly. Unfortunately, my old method of disappearing bitter vegetables or gristly meat failed me in this instance. Tom's little sinkers were unflushable.

Never wanting to waste anything, Tom aimed to put a chicken carcass to good use one morning by boiling it down for stock. He dialed the electric burner up to high.

That's when the phone rang. And like a squirrel attracted to a shiny object, he impetuously accepted an offer to go visit a friend, completely forgetting the project he'd started. By the time he got home that afternoon, the top third of the house was filled with smoke, and everything in it reeked like burnt chicken feathers.

We made the mistake of coming to town to help clean up that weekend, which was too soon. The stink wasn't done permeating the space, and it all came back. We were obliged to repeat the process the following week. Some things, like John's Italian leather jacket, never did recover.

Bearing in mind these incidents, we thought we'd keep Dad out of the house and on the road as much as possible. Our place was a rental for which we'd paid a hefty *kaution*. It's a peculiarity of German renters that they begin to think of this breakage deposit as theirs, and no matter how long and congenial the business relationship, they will find excuses to keep it when you move out. We didn't want Tom to give our landlord a good reason for keeping this money.

Since I didn't require caffeine, and John got his from Diet Mountain Dew, we never owned a coffeemaker. Before Tom arrived, we bought a plastic funnel, brown paper filters, and richly nutty Jacobs Kronung grounds, so he could brew a cupful as weak or as strong as he wished, as early in the morning as he liked. The process was definitely low-tech. The coffee was already ground. There was no steaming, percolating, pressing, foaming, or squirting. Just heat and pour. We never could figure out how he managed to splatter coffee on the kitchen ceiling.

~I~

GOURMET OR GOURMAND?

My father-in-law enjoyed whatever life had to offer, particularly after he retired. Tom would try anything. Eat anything.

One time in Arizona, he was clearing grassland for some horse property when he unearthed a plant with a tuber-like root. It resembled a potato closely enough that he wondered if it might be edible. It was, but he couldn't make the drive home without a couple of urgent stops. On a road not known for roadside rest areas.

"You're quite the gourmand," I told him. He was flattered until I pointed out that gourmand is not the same thing as gourmet. A gourmet is a connoisseur, a person of refined tastes who knows and appreciates fine wines and exotic comestibles. A gourmand, on the other hand, simply likes food. A lot. I thought Tom qualified since he regularly remarked that his favorite meal ever was the one he'd just finished eating.

He was adventurous, but not everything tempted him, to my surprise. In France's Loire Valley, he literally turned up his nose at the region's famous Crottin de Chavignol, a full-flavored goat cheese. He marveled that I would eat it because I had not always liked his distinctive preparations:

smoked pork, smoked beef, smoked fish, barbecued ribs, pork cracklings, too-hot Mexican sauces.

"And yet you like this cheese?"

I did. I would eat escargot and frogs' legs too. In America, it would never occur to me to eat snails. In France, it would. It's kind of like wearing an itchy wool sweater. You can do it, but you have to psych yourself up for it.

Tom could smell the soft, odiferous cheese when it arrived at the table, and it was one of few foods in his life he declined to try. He had grown up on a farm and knew what a goat barn smelled like. It smelled like that cheese.

On this trip, Tom had arrived two days after Christmas. There wasn't a lot of hiking we could do with him in the wintry weather of central Germany. Some of the drives might be dreary and gray, but we decided to take him to the Loire Valley to visit some French châteaux. Though the gardens were dry and brown, the massive structures looked impressive any time of year, and much of the visiting was indoors anyway.

We drove him to Azay-le-Rideau, whose sixteenth century architecture Honoré de Balzac had described as a diamond with a thousand facets, built on pilasters, perched on an island in the Indre River. We bypassed my beloved Villandry on this trip because its nine exquisite, geometrical vegetable gardens, bordered by fruit trees, were bland in winter dormancy. Le Château de Chenonceau left a lasting impression with its arched bridge built in the mid-sixteenth century to connect the castle to the opposite bank of the Cher River. Le Château de Chambord featured expansive terraces and spiral staircases due to the influence of Leonardo da Vinci. It had 282 fireplaces, one in each apartment. (We did not see them all.) We climbed to the top, gaining access to the roof terrace, where visitors typically surveyed a grand view of the valley. What we experienced that day was different: thick, cool fog that silenced our footsteps, muffled our voices, and softened silhouettes into a scene worthy of a Guillaume Vogels landscape. Exiting the sixteenth century château, we passed through narrow stone walls and overheard a small group speaking English. Our English, not British English.

"Hey, there's some more Americans," Tom exclaimed.

"We're from Canada."

"Well now... American, Canadian. Practically the same thing," Tom said.

We pretended not to know him.

Not many places were open for dinner in Tours over the holidays. We found an informal restaurant, almost a diner, where most of the menu items were salads. The one I ordered became the inspiration for recipes I would later prepare for special guests. An oval platter was spread with crisp, large-leaved greens and generously topped with grilled lardons and morsels of a soft, almost fluffy bleu cheese, breaded and pan-fried. One of most memorable meals I've enjoyed in my life. If I'm not mistaken, Tom remarked that it was the best salad he'd ever had.

The last night of the year, we were still in Tours. Of course, it's not Paris, but let's see how folks in this region ring in the new year.

They don't.

No lights or decorations on the town square. Not a strain of music leaking through an opened door. No couples in elegant evening wear setting out in taxis to party until morning. No one anywhere. Even at midnight, not so much as a horn or firecracker. Nothing. No sign anywhere that it might be a holiday. It was the quietest New Year's Eve I've ever spent. And I've lived in some small, dull places.

Tours: It's probably a nice place to live, but I wouldn't want to visit there.

ളȷᴗ

TWO AUNTIES IN THE BACK SEAT

I t was the era when men saved money all their lives for retirement, and then died so their wives could go on cruises and safaris. Aunt Mildred was a widow for four decades, so she got to travel to Europe, South America, and Africa. Aunt Frances had a dear husband whose kind personality and keen intellect were slowly robbed by Alzheimer's Disease, after which she was free to fulfill a dream of going to Europe. She came to see us in Germany.

Having visitors prompted us to do things that were on our go-see list anyway – or things that should've been. I lived in Idaho for a decade without feeling compelled to visit the potato museum before my sister-in-law arrived with her wish list. I could swear she took a picture of every exhibit in the place. The only exhibit that stuck in my mind was on loan from the Basque Museum. It was an excerpt of a letter written by an aging shepherd who had found the adjustment from northern Spain to desolate Idaho arduous: "I hate to think of my children and grandchildren dying in this God-forsaken place."

In Europe were many places we hoped to visit. Besides, I owed my aunt a debt of gratitude for welcoming this small-town girl to stay with her in the big city of Phoenix every summer of my childhood. Showing her around Europe would accomplish multiple ends.

My aunt said she'd like to bring a companion, and we thought this plan would relieve us of the responsibility for entertaining her all the time. So there we were with a couple of octogenarians in the back seat of our blue Mitsubishi Gallant. Reinhardt had helped us buy a *jahreswagen*. This is an automobile less than a year old that has only been rented by little *alte Frauen* to get to church on Sundays.

My aunt wanted to see Paris and the Heidelberg castle on the Neckar River and the Black Forest and the Alps. Anything we were willing to drive to. Her friend Edie's one expressed wish was to dine on genuine Italian spaghetti. In Italy. That sounds doable, right?

The two visitors packed as we had advised: appropriate layers of clothing, comfortable shoes, and rain gear. My aunt's umbrella was bright pink, and it fell apart the first time she opened it. She'd probably had it in a closet in Phoenix for thirty years waiting for it to rain. Eventually, the synthetic fabric had dried out and split. I laughed and outfitted her with a Knirps automatic designed with a handle to slide up and pop open at the push of a button.

We booked rooms across Germany, France, Switzerland, and Italy. Breakfast was always included. Normally I don't eat in the morning, but if my reservation offers *petit déjeuner compris,* you can bet I'll show up. Then I do everything possible to embarrass my husband, like tucking an apple, some cheese, and an extra croissant into my purse. *Croissants pur beurre* made with real butter.

Back home, my friends would serve the Poppin' Fresh version that came out of a roll you whacked on the counter until it scared you, the kind that you had to roll up from triangles of refrigerated dough. They didn't taste like the ones in France. That would be owing largely to the "pure butter" part of the description. However, I sometimes told people it was because they didn't adequately curve the ends of the pastry on the cookie sheet. *Croissant* means crescent. How can they taste heavenly if they're not shaped like the moon?

The aunties were content with the morning buffets of breads, fresh butter, fruit preserves, soft-boiled eggs, sliced meats, and cheeses. A hearty beginning to the day. Except for the coffee. Small cups of dark, opaque brown, heavy on caffeine.

"Oh my, it's so strong!" Frances gasped. Edie agreed. It was strong and bitter, and they could scarcely drink it. Before asking for refills.

The next morning, same routine. "The coffee's too strong."

"Would you prefer tea? Or hot cocoa?"

No. They drank coffee every morning. And marveled at its intensity every morning.

Evening meals presented their own challenges. The ladies enjoyed schnitzel. They liked *gulaschsuppe*. Sauerbraten. Sauerkraut. German potatoes were the tastiest they'd ever had. The salads were fresh and colorful surprises with lettuce varieties unfamiliar to us. And then there was the bread. A basket might have slices of rye or thick chunks of baguette. Crusty outside, soft inside, baked fresh that day.

"Where's the butter? Did you get any butter?"

"No, I don't see any either."

"There's no butter."

Every time we had dinner out. After a while, they could tell we were tired of explaining that butter was not served with bread at dinner. So they quit asking for it. That is, they quit asking *us*. But we could hear them whispering to each other: "I don't see any butter, do you?" "Why don't they ever serve butter?"

Every morning. The coffee's too strong.

Every evening. Where's the butter?

Two weeks, and they never got over it.

One thing I'll say in their favor. Without fail, these little ladies were ready in the morning, no matter what departure time John set. Compact suitcases were buttoned up. They checked out on time, didn't forget anything in their rooms. They were always standing at the curb in front of the hotel, ready to get into the back seat of our sedan for a long day of riding, sitting, climbing in and out, and sightseeing. We drove them through green pastures and villages in France, into the Black Forest to buy cuckoo clocks, and up and down vineyard-covered hills, through tunnels and mountains in Switzerland, where they got to watch craftsmen at a *freilichtmuseum*.

Getting to the open-air museum entailed taking a series of country side roads and getting there by midafternoon before the exhibits closed for the day. We were all happily anticipating walking among seventeenth-century thatch-roofed barns and half-timbered chalets with their steep-pitched roofs and overhanging upper floors. Our two charges in the back seat were consulting their guidebooks and describing the features they were most eager to see: The cobbler and blacksmith in period dress. The sawmill, the distillery, the stone kitchen oven, and the organic herb gardens. Demonstrations of traditional basket weaving, wood carving, and cheesemaking.

John set the schedule, but I was the designated navigator. Big mistake. I was following a Falk flip-and-fold map as our vehicle hurtled along shaded paths through pastureland, and I was trying to identify passing villages and unnamed roads. There was no one-to-one correlation between towns on the ground and names on the map. The scale confused me, so I didn't know if we were coming upon a certain intersection or if that was the one we'd just passed. "Wait. Stop. Make a U-turn. Oh, no, never mind, keep going. Sorry."

"Well, which is it?"

The back-seat chatter grew quieter.

"We're gonna be too late." Husband pulled over by an irrigation ditch to check things out for himself.

"Can't you read a map?"

Dead silence from the aunties. Awkward, dead silence.

Ultimately we made it to the fascinating museum. As we were stepping out of the car, Aunt Frances leaned in close to me: "It's all right, dear. Don't worry about it. The worst argument I ever had with your Uncle Paul was about driving somewhere and getting lost."

Our last goal was to get Edie to her priority destination. A quick dip into northern Italy was all we'd have time for. Val d'Aosta with its alpine views.

John identified a small but highly recommended restaurant with old stone walls and a balcony view. There we relished one of the most memorable meals of our travels. Prosciutto di Parma, rice dishes with seafood in creamy white sauces rich in clarified butter, fish with savory herbs. Valpolicella to drink. Panna cotta for dessert.

We were serenaded by a middle-aged violinist with a pale pink shirt, a balding head, and a pleasant face. He asked if we had any favorite songs, and John's request was, "Please play one of your favorites that no ever requests." Charming. The musician loved him for it. Score points, John.

The only problem was no pasta, no tomato-red marinara sauce.

All things considered, it was the trip of a lifetime for the aunties. They could hardly have been more gracious. If it had been a baseball game, we might have scored a home run.

We showed our visitors the Alps, the Rhine, the City of Light.

Bases are loaded.

They'd visited the Louvre, entered castles filled with medieval armor, and viewed fifty-foot-high stained-glass windows in cathedrals while the pipe organist was practicing.

Opportunity for a grand slam.

They'd taken a cogwheel train and seen the dazzling 14,690 foot Matterhorn on a clear day.

It's a hit.

We'd had sumptuous meals, fabulous wines, and desserts almost too pretty to eat.

Rounding third base.

But we failed to find Italian spaghetti with tomato sauce.

Tag out!

ᖾᕽ

ON HER OWN

When I met Cassandra, I thought she was a recent college grad visiting an older and wiser sister whose husband was stationed at Ramstein Air Base. A stabilizing influence on a twenty-year-old hiking around with a backpack and a Eurail Pass? In fact, the sister was younger, active duty, and subject to being transferred soon. Cassie was quite stable and purposeful on her own: she'd boarded a plane bound from Baltimore to Frankfurt with a freshly minted university diploma and a polished résumé. My department hired her as a writer immediately. She was competent and energetic and got along with colleagues of all ages. One department head would fondly describe some of her outfits as "over-matched" when her headband, earrings, and socks were all the same color, be it mustard gold or shocking pink or vibrant turquoise.

She found and rented an apartment with a balcony on a quiet street not far from our offices, and a college friend moved in with her. Bianca got a job on an army base, and it wasn't long before men in uniform became enamored with the two attractive blondes. One day an admirer drove a huge green tank down their residential road to impress them. I wonder how the neighbors felt about that.

From the perspective of the young women, it was all strictly platonic, but the friendships were helpful in accomplishing some tasks. Such as dragging upstairs an old bathtub with cabriole legs. They spotted it on bulk-trash day, a time when homeowners set on the sidewalk used furniture, appliances, or rugs for pickup. The custom was to put things out a day in advance so passersby could help themselves and keep useful objects from going straight to the dump. The roomies thought it was a fantastically fun find; they painted it purple and filled it with pillows.

One morning, Cassandra rode to work on her bike while listening to Mireille Mathieu on her bright-yellow Walkman. In the public relations office, she held her earphones up to my ear, and the pumping whir of the Heidelberg press receded. *"Pardonne-Moi Ce Caprice d'Enfant"* was on, and I was back in high school playing and replaying the vinyl records Mémé would send from Paris, trying to catch the lyrics and learn all the French words.

The next morning, Cassie was listening to the Beatles. "I just love classical music," she teased. The morning after that, she didn't show up at all. Her roommate, Bianca, let me know Cassie had been in a bicycle collision. Coming home the previous evening, she had huffed and puffed her way uphill on the used bike and then, as usual, relaxed while coasting down her street and into the driveway that wound around her apartment. Nearing the parking area, she squeezed the brake with her left hand. This time the cable snapped.

The bike picked up speed. Faster and faster, and then she couldn't stop. As she was crashing into the neighbor's low cement wall and flipping headfirst over the handlebars, Bianca called from the kitchen window, "Use the pedal brake!" Just before landing on her back, Cassie cried out, "There's a pedal brake?"

ON THE ROAD AND ON HER WAY

In the gushing impulse that accompanies farewells, I invited everyone we knew to come visit us. As far away as we were going, there was little risk that too many would oblige, but occasionally I wondered what would happen if they all arrived at once. We had a 900-square-foot apartment with two bedrooms. One served as master bedroom, and the other was filled with wardrobes. As it turned out, we only had visitors a couple times, and their sunny Arizona faces were welcome sights in our doorway.

One summer, K.T. spent a few days with us during her thorough tour of Europe. She was my friend's younger sibling, and we'd all taken a dance class together when she was about eighteen. A bright student, she was mulling over a range of career options.

"I either want to study electrical engineering or go to clown school," she announced. It was kind of up in the air. By the time spring semester began, engineering had won the coin toss. One afternoon, K.T. called mysteriously from her college dorm to make sure her mother was home; she needed to talk. She caught a ride from campus and sat by her mom on the sofa to announce, "Mom, I've been jumping out of airplanes." A fellow student had talked her into taking a skydiving class, then backed out at the last minute, but K.T. put on the parachute and followed through with her commitment. After the jump, she decided she had better fess up to her parents before someone else broke the news for her.

This was the girl who was coming to see us.

In the intervening years, K.T. had finished college and begun working on a master's degree. After the years of formal classroom requirements were completed, and before writing her thesis, K.T. decided to clear her mind by spending a summer traveling abroad. The classic college-completion capstone experience. Her plan was to take BritRail around England, then rendezvous with a college acquaintance in Amsterdam to complete the summer's extensive itinerary. After spending a night in a Dutch youth hostel that got raided by police, she called us from the Frankfurt airport to say the friend had never shown up, but she had resolutely decided to visit the continent on her own, so we advised her concerning train routes and went to pick her up.

She was wearing shorts and tennis shoes, her arms and legs already deeply tanned and her short hair sun-bleached. An army-surplus frame pack covered her back. Its primary contents were a sleeping bag and a copy of *Let's Go, Europe*. There were shorts and jeans and several blouses and a backup pair of walking shoes. The skirt, K.T. said, she had not needed. She had a camera but said she wasn't taking many pictures or purchasing postcards, except to send to her parents. She was faithfully making entries in a diary, however.

When she needed clean laundry, K.T. did some handwash at a youth hostel and, since things were rarely dry by morning, she hung them on ropes across the pack and let her clothes dry as she walked. It was classic college-kid hoofing, a scene right out of the sixties. I did not confess to this intrepid child that I was afraid of getting lost on the way to the PX or that I couldn't sleep at night when I was home alone.

So, what would this independent young woman most like to see in this part of the world?

"Oh, I don't know." She was noncommittal.

Any particular foods you like or castles you've read about?

"Anything's all right."

We went to Heidelberg Castle on the Neckar River and to the 1868 Luther Monument in Worms. We took her to *sommerfest* in Pfiffligheim. German friends of ours took her bowling and introduced her to boating on an artificial lake. They were charmed by our visitor and gave her a porcelain figurine as a remembrance. She sampled bratwurst and schnitzel, had a stein of Pilsner, and sipped a glass of Liebfraumilch. After two or three days, K.T. thought she should continue her adventure. She was still to meet Swiss cousins who took the train to school every day. She had to visit castles, cathedrals, art galleries, and museums to the point that they all blurred together. To her credit, she paid her respects at such sobering sites as war memorials and Dachau concentration camp. She would face challenges making change in Marseille on Bastille Day, get her money stolen in Spain, and take her Eurail Pass as far south as Estrela, Portugal. It's a good thing we couldn't foresee some of these adventures when she left.

Reluctantly we drove K.T. back to the Heidelberg Hauptbahnhof. Wearing khaki shorts, a red *Mutter Erde Tag* T-shirt celebrating Earth Day, and the huge backpack, she thanked us and headed for the platform to catch a southbound train. She looked so little and so young that I got a lump in my throat watching her recede into the crowd.

᠁ I ᠁

GOING BACK

YOU REALLY LIVE HERE WHEN YOU START ATTENDING FUNERALS

Military brats have wanderlust in their blood. Like Laura Ingalls' father on the prairie, they get restless to move on every couple of years. I'd lived in the same place for twenty years and didn't understand why my spouse wanted to change residences so often. He came by it naturally. His father had served the army in Kansas, Georgia, Texas, California, Illinois, New Jersey, Japan, Korea, the Philippines, and the Panama Canal Zone. Next he moved his family to the American Southwest when he retired. Even then he kept changing locations: rental house, purchased home, horse property.

Like many college students, John would go visit his parents every few weekends to share a homecooked meal and get his laundry done. Before school started his sophomore year, he helped his father and step-mother move from one house to another house across town. He loaded and unloaded furniture all Saturday and Sunday from a four-horse trailer. After the first week of classes, he drove back home so he could work one last weekend lifeguarding at the city pool. When he pulled up to the new driveway, there was his dad packing up the four-horse trailer at the house he had just moved into.

"We got a great deal on some horse property south of town. Glad you're back today to help us move again, Son."

That weekend, too, he helped his parents take everything they owned from one house to another. The weekend after that, he stayed on campus.

It became a favorite anecdote, but it was really nothing extraordinary. Your parents move; you help them. You do it for friends making military moves too. This assures that furniture gets adequately padded, electronics don't get stolen, and kitchen garbage doesn't get boxed and shipped.

***

Rarely would an American come to know European civilians well enough to help them move from one city to another. We had that privilege and that responsibility after befriending a French doctoral student at Syracuse University. When we moved to Europe, we got acquainted with her parents and had occasion to visit them while she was still in the U.S. They were highly educated, well read, and politically informed. They were also devout Catholics who engaged us in discussions of religion, politics, and philosophy. Estelle's father tried to interest us in chess and insisted we visit nearby Collonges-la-Rouge, an eighth-century village built entirely of red sandstone. It was one of those precious phases in life when we got acquainted with people a generation older than we to such an extent that they became our friends, not just parents of friends. We were to share unanticipated joy and pain with them.

It was uncharacteristic for French families to uproot themselves often, but Estelle's parents followed opportunities for jobs in engineering and teaching, and they moved again upon retirement, first to their old hometown and then to be nearer their grown children. Two years after Estelle's younger sister married a library archivist who accepted a job in Limoges, her parents decided to move somewhat closer to them and their newest grandchild. After much consideration and research, they selected a home about four hours' drive away, in Nantes, where her mother could do errands on foot and her father could walk to Mass every day.

It was late autumn when we volunteered to help them box up their possessions in preparation for an upcoming move from Saverne, on the far northeast side of France, to Nantes, on the far west side. My primary task was to pack the books. A previous professional mover had complained about their having so many *bouquins*, an informal term for "little book." Although she was a woman without pretentions, Odile had found the reference slightly insulting. What they owned were *livres*, a more formal word appropriate to most of their collection. Possessions worth keeping and moving. My packing was slowed by my curiosity about the titles of novels, detective stories, children's series and comics like *Lucky Luke,* and numerous books about social and political issues. Not many U.S. civil servants gain such intimate entry into European homes. Yet we had this chance, not only in Germany, where we worked, but in France, my mother's homeland. How lucky we were.

On a dreary November day, we got a phone call from the U.S., a doctoral student from John and Estelle's cohort. There'd been a tragic collision in France. Estelle's sister had been walking at dusk from her new home to a meeting of parents at the child-care center. Crossing a small highway at dusk, she'd been struck by a speeding car and killed.

As friends in New York helped Estelle make international flight arrangements, we drove to Limoges to attend the funeral to which Estelle wore a green dress, symbolic of her belief in eternal life. Some days after the funeral Mass, we drove her parents from Limoges to Saverne to complete their move to Nantes. Once in a while, we'd hear "Ça va?" from the back seat as Odile fretted about whether her fatigued driver was alert. "Ça va?" Is everything OK?

Several months later, we would help them pack up the same books and clothing and dishes to move from Nantes to an apartment in Limoges, where they would spend years helping to rear their grandson.

Christophe was barely a year old when he lost his mother. He had no idea what was going on. All he knew was that the most significant presence in his life had disappeared. In the night, when he would awaken and cry as babies do, Estelle or her mother would get up and go to his crib to comfort him. He'd pause in his crying when the bedroom door opened, then start wailing anew when he saw she was not the right person. This pierced their hearts because they knew what he wanted, and they could not give it to him. During the day every time the front door opened, he would glance up eagerly and begin toddling toward the entrance, only to realize some other adult had entered the house. Not the woman he was looking for.

I don't know which was more sad: the little fellow continually watching for his mother week after week, or the day he quit expecting her to return.

༄·!·༄

UNE HISTOIRE D'AMOUR

French was not spoken in our home except when Mother was praying, swearing, or doing math. She claimed she was too homesick to teach my brother and me her first language, but there was a practical reason too. The French my dad could speak consisted of a few phrases he fractured to comic effect. The French women we met locally were war brides. They had married men who'd served in France during World War II and had a chance to pick up some French – and some French women.

My mother had an American father. After the war, she came to Washington, DC looking for him. That's where she met my father. The only time he had been in France was at Utah Beach. As a U.S. Navy medic, he approached the bluffs to retrieve wounded and dead servicemen. Not quite the moment for learning noun genders and verb conjugations.

With little background in French other than the constant example of her bona fide accent, we were obliged to study the language when we entered high school. My brother was brighter than I but, in this subject, I displayed either more aptitude or more interest.

My Parisian grandmother was delighted to learn that I was applying myself to the discipline. She began sending me vinyl records of singers popular in France at that time.

Hervé Vilard. Rika Zaraï. Mireille Mathieu. Grandmother spent from her modest pension, painstakingly padded and wrapped the records in brown paper, and shipped them across the sea, keeping track of which titles she'd already sent me to avoid duplicating gifts over time. On a portable stereo with a diamond needle, I'd play every song repeatedly, understanding perhaps one new word with each repetition. I began transcribing them and would ask my mother when I didn't understand something. They were mostly love songs, and she'd roll her eyes when asked to translate anything too romantic.

Mathieu was hailed as the next Édith Piaf and became a huge star, recording a thousand songs. Sitting on my bedroom floor, I'd write down the lyrics in lead pencil, lifting and dropping the needle a dozen times to try to catch a particular phrase. I could never have imagined that I'd meet a woman who knew the singer and would gift me albums of her work. A German woman. Connie's son had been the artist's publicity manager and recruited her to reply to enthusiastic Germans who were writing fan mail to Mireille. My collection of records from France would eventually be augmented by 33 RPMs with album covers autographed in blue marker by the chanteuse herself.

When Connie died, we had no hesitation about going to pay our respects. What did give me pause was being expected to take a turn shoveling dirt onto her coffin.

If you know local nationals well enough to get invited to family weddings, it's a privilege. If you know them well enough to attend family funerals, it's a duty. We've attended several of each in more than one country and culture.

A short reception followed Connie's burial. I noticed mourners at the restaurant leaving envelopes for the deceased's granddaughter. I did likewise, placing a condolence card in the basket by the exit. Later I learned that the other envelopes contained money to defray the costs of the meal. Another gap in my knowledge of local customs. Another gaffe.

~I~

THE WOLF DOG

Never go empty-handed. It was a French rule, inculcated by my Parisian mother. Any time we were invited to someone's home, she would come up with a hostess gift "to offer them." Not take or give. Offer. Dad found it funny that she translated directly from her native idiom. It's not as though the hostess can very well refuse it, he'd point out.

Following her example, we tried to be considerate houseguests. Arrive with flowers or some sort of treat. Remove our shoes at the door. Help with the dishes.

It was nice of Volker and Diane to invite us to stay with them for a couple of nights right before we returned to the States. The movers and inspectors had come and gone. Our household goods had begun their voyage across the Atlantic Ocean. One piece of furniture would be scraping back and forth against another at twenty knots per hour, creating sawdust with every wave of the sea. What remained in the apartment, we carted over to Volker's place in the trunk of our car and spent an entire day upstairs packing and repacking into four suitcases.

After that, it seemed only fitting that we should help with household chores like walking the dog. A big dog that had earned its name, Monster, on the day it arrived by poaching a week's worth of *vollkornbrot* off the kitchen counter and gulping it down in a few minutes. By the time Diane and Volker realized what he'd done, the fibrous bread was working its way through the hound's digestive tract – and beyond.

OK, so they asked us to walk the dog. It was nice out. Monster had a good, strong leash. We walked the dog. As this was evening exercise for us all, we conscientiously kept moving. If Monster wanted to keep stopping to sniff things, we corrected him and tugged at his leash, goading him further along the block.

"How did it go?"

"Great. It was a fine walk." John hung the leash on a coatrack in the foyer.

At that moment, the dog peed all over the entryway floor, making a huge puddle. *Oh. Walking doesn't just mean walking? Why didn't y'all say so?*

Thank goodness that wasn't the day Monster had consumed the wholegrain bread.

Quite satisfied with ourselves and having done our good deeds for the day, we bade our hosts an early goodnight and went up to the *dachwohnung*. John had hurt his back helping to move furniture and was suffering spasms, for which codeine had been prescribed. He was hoping to find some relief before we had to start an eight-hour plane ride in coach class.

The bedding was soft and cozy. I'd been sound asleep for hours when he shook me awake.

"Get up! Get up! Get out of bed! There's a big spider!" Germany has some hellacious spiders with dark thick bodies, and they like to build webs beneath the windowsills under the geraniums. A huge black spider was descending from the ceiling, John cried out, practically pushing me off the other side of the bed to escape.

In the morning, rather than the customary, "Did you sleep well?" our hosts couldn't resist asking about the 2 a.m. ruckus that had turned out to be a nightmare.

No more codeine for you, sir.

◦!◦

TWO PHONE CALLS

The move was precipitated by a phone call.

The telephone was in the hall; when it rang in the middle of the night, I ran stumbling through the darkness to grab the receiver and hush its insistent jangling. A frantic chorus raced from my brain to my heart. *What's wrong? What's wrong? Who calls at this hour unless there's something wrong?*

A vacuous silence on the line told me not to hang up, that this was not a prank nor a wrong number but a long-distance connection.

Mother was in the hospital having surgery. Not many details were offered.

I wanted to be there. Should I fly home immediately? John was out of town, so I paced about the flat, trying to decide what to do.

After he got back, the phone rang again, earlier in the evening this time. Another call from the USA. It was a job offer back in our hometown. He said he'd think about it. His current work was fulfilling, and we didn't feel like we were finished experiencing Europe. Curtailing our stint abroad, we might never take the Mediterranean cruise that topped John's travel wish list. We hadn't seen the fjords of Norway or traced my father's roots in Czechoslovakia.

What limited vacation time we had we'd largely spent in Paris getting acquainted with my mother's family, relatives I'd never met during my childhood.

What about those exotic islands and far-away cities from my old record albums? There was so much more of Europe than we had experienced. If we left now, would we ever see it? We'd fallen in love with people and places. We'd begun considering whether to extend our tour of duty when renewal time arrived – if we could figure out how to break the news to our parents. And now, suddenly, I was ready to turn my back on all of it.

While my husband weighed his career options, in my mind we were already on an airplane headed home. I had us half-packed before he'd made his decision.

Please, John, this is meant to be. It's too much of a coincidence otherwise.

He consented, and we began making arrangements.

Normally I'd have felt sad leaving our German abode. Overly sentimental, I'd have taken a final glance around the apartment to bid each room farewell.

But I didn't.

I left with barely a glance backward.

My parents needed me. I was going home.

It didn't occur to me until later that there might have been less dramatic alternatives. Or that one day I might return.

FIN

AUTHOR'S BIOGRAPHY

MARTINE ROBINSON BEACHBOARD

The author has loved words since she first learned about them. This occurred when, at the age of 2, she spent a week with her older brother in the hot, sticky backseat of the green Ford her parents drove from Washington, D.C. to Phoenix. She studied enough words to win a citywide spelling bee in seventh grade. Next thing you know, she was a newspaper editor in Arizona. Her weekly personal column developed a loyal following and evoked a range of reader responses and emotions.

When she moved to Europe she continued writing. She has lived or traveled in 40 countries, most recently serving as a Fulbright Scholar in Kosovo.

She was awarded first place in column writing from the Arizona Press Club. Her editing has been recognized with four first-place awards by Arizona Press Women. A Penney-Missouri Newspaper Awards competition named her a finalist in single-story reporting. A former professor, she is currently a teacher of English as a Second Language.

Early in her journalism career, she learned that everyone has a story. With increased interviewing experience, she realized that everyone *is* a story.

www.ingramcontent.com/pod-product-compliance
Lightning Source LLC
Chambersburg PA
CBHW061605120626
46550CB00004B/1619